THE CATHEDRAL OF OUR LADY in Antwerp

THE CATHEDRAL OF OUR LADY in Antwerp

Jan Van Damme

Kathedrale kerkfabriek
Onze-Lieve-Vrouw Antwerpen

Snoeck-Ducaju & Zoon

Table of contents

When we first enter this cathedral our mind turns inexorably to the countless people who have been here before us over the centuries: people like you and me who have lived through their own chapter of human history. Homo viator, the man on a journey, has often come here to seek comfort and fresh inspiration. There have been many reasons for coming to the cathedral: simple curiosity, the powerful attraction of certain works of art, sights that people want to see close up. Many visitors come here to look deep into themselves, to seek peace and God. They come into contact with a knowledge that makes us more human, simply by opening ourselves to the sacred spirit of this place, an atmosphere that invites us to contemplate and to pray.

The works of art which adorn this church and which you can still admire today were in the past the means of expressing the relationship between Man and God, whose house this building is. People use ritual, symbols and allegory to give visual form to what is sacred. Artistic beauty allows us to externalize a reality which can only be achieved by internalization in contemplation and prayer. The unique feature of religious art is that it flows from the depths of our spiritual life and our religious emotions. It is not bound to the past: people of all eras can experience it. This is why the cathedral is not a museum. It is a dwelling used for liturgical services and prayer. It calls on us, as on so many before us, to spend a few moments in repentance. I hope that you will find it a morally uplifting experience.

Canon Omer HAMELS
Pastor and Dean of the cathedral
Dean of Central Antwerp

'God is well housed in his good city of Antwerp'

R. AVERMAETE

Churches are sensitive places. Their history runs through the development of a city. In times of prosperity they are rebuilt and modernized and in times of civil disorder they are not spared. The story of a cathedral has something to tell not just about the past of a particular city but about the broader sweep of history. It is a story of people and bears the traces of their experience: from the times when the Church was the centre of their world, all music was church music, the history of the plastic arts was written on the church porch and on the altars, the church tower was a focal point around which the city grew like a living thing and by which the city could be recognized from afar, up to modern times when society has become more secular and some churches are visited more by tourists than believers and contemporary religious art has more or less disappeared.

Over all this time the building has been strikingly adaptable. Though its importance has risen and fallen over the years, the Church of Our Lady has always been a significant place and its history is a source of fascination to many. Its exact origins are still unclear even today. We know that Saint Eligius (ca. 590-ca. 660) came to 'Andoverpis' to try to convert the barbarian 'Andoverpenses'. Saint Amand made another attempt soon afterwards and founded the Church of Saint Peter and Saint Paul on the Chanelaus islet near the River Schelde. Some people think that Chanelaus is a derivation of Kallo, a village on the Schelde not far from Antwerp, but there is more support for the view that Chanelaus is the old Caloes, an area of higher ground running alongside the river to the south of the town. Towards the end of the seventh century the Church of Saint Peter and Saint Paul was given to Saint Willibrord by Rohingus, a Frankish nobleman. Saint Willibrord gave it to the Abbey of Echternach which he had founded. For many years it was thought that this early place of worship was the forerunner of the old Church of Saint Walburga, named after the saint who, according to legend, lived in the crypt for some time in the middle of the eighth century before founding a convent in Hildesheim (Bavaria). This is why the back of the external panels of the Rubens triptych depicting the Raising of the Cross, which is now in the cathedral but comes from the Church of Saint Walburga, show Saint Eligius and Saint Amand in the company of Saint Walburga. Archeologists have now discovered that the Church of Saint Walburga was probably not founded until the tenth century. Its foundation can be linked to the decree of Otto the Second, just before 980, to create a shire with a castle on the Scheldt to defend his lands. Since the Treaty of Verdun (843) the river had always formed the boundary between France and Lorraine. This means that we must seek elsewhere to find the oldest church in Antwerp. The search is made more difficult by the fact that the settlement was laid waste by the Normans in 836. Another possible successor to the Church of Saint Peter and Saint Paul is the old Church of Saint Michael, south of the castle near the old Caloes. It was the parish church of Antwerp until 1124 and had authority over the Church of Saint Walburga and a Chapel of Our Lady that then lay outside the town walls.

Legend has it that Godfried de Bouillon, the margrave of Antwerp, made his crusader's vows on Christmas night in 1096 in the previously unknown Church of Our Lady. The first reliable references to the church come in 1124 when it was elevated to the status of a parish church by Bishop Burchard of Cambrai. The reason for its elevation was the conversion of the

Left:
PETER PAUL RUBENS
Saints Eligius, Walburga, Amand and Catherine, outer panels of the triptych *Raising of the Cross*, 1610

QUOD AMANDUS INCHOARAT, QUOD ELIGIUS PLANTARAT, WILLEBRORDUS IRRIGARAT, TANCHELINUS DEVASTARAT, NORBERTUS RESTITUIT.

ABRAHAM VAN DIEPENBEEK,
Saint Norbert,
17th century

chapter of St. Michael's Church, the parish church of Antwerp, into a Norbertine abbey. Nothing is known of when the oldest Church of Our Lady was built or what it looked like, but the circumstances under which the reorganization took place are of some interest. The most picturesque role in the story is certainly that of the alleged heretic Tanchelm, who had accused the existing church and some of the clergy of all kinds of abuses. If we are to believe the Chapter of Utrecht, Tanchelm preached against the sacraments, especially the Eucharist, and incited the faithful to stop paying tithes. He announced his betrothal to an image of the

Virgin Mary and was intimate with mothers and daughters. The Utrecht canons claimed that some people drank his bath water out of veneration. Bishop Burchard of Cambrai, the diocese responsible for Antwerp, sent his friend Saint Norbert to Antwerp to suppress the activities of his followers. Norbert took firm control of the situation and introduced a radical reorganization, converting the old St. Michael's Church into a Norbertine monastery and making the Church of Our Lady the new parish church for Antwerp. For this reason Saint Norbert enjoys special veneration to this day in the former Abbey of Saint Michael and in the Church

JOSEPHUS I HENNEKIN,
Torch guard, 1699-1700

of Our Lady. He is invariably depicted as the saint who restored respect for the Holy Sacrament of the Eucharist and conquered Tanchelm's heresy. A portrait painted by Abraham van Diepenbeek (1596-1675) is inscribed: 'Quod Amand inchoarat / Quod Eligius plantarat / Willibrord irrigarat / Tanchelmus devastarat / Norbertus restituit' (What was started by Amand, planted by Eligius and watered by Willibrord, devastated by Tanchelmus, was restored by Norbertus). Norbert was held in particular honour by the fraternity of the Holy Sacrament or Venerable. We do not know exactly when the fraternity was founded, but it must have been before 1446. Its members were citizens who worked to achieve greater devotion to and respect for the sacrament of the Eucharist. With this aim in view they erected a special chapel in the south side aisle of the church and provided furnishings and services for its altar. One of the articles they supplied was the silver-gilt ciborium dating from 1664-1665 made by the goldsmith Hendrick Corbion who came originally from Liège but had by then settled in Antwerp. It is used to take the sacrament to the sick and is highly decorated with subjects relating to the Eucharist, such as the manna from heaven, the wedding at Cana and the men of Emmaus. Ornaments of this kind were usually given by members of the fraternity; this was probably also the case of the torch guard made by the silversmith Josephus I Hennekin, himself a member of the chapel of the Venerable, in 1699-1700. The chalice and the host shown on the shield are clear references to the Eucharist. The fraternity was abolished during the French Revolution, but was later restored and is still active today, contributing to the splendour of services in the cathedral.

Fragments of the Roman place of worship

The guild of the Holy Sacrament was not the only and certainly not the oldest fraternity housed in the Church of Our Lady. As early as 1282 a chaplaincy served by two chaplains was founded at the altar of the Holy Cross: one chaplain read the Mass of the Holy Cross every other day, while the other read a Mass for the Dead on Mondays, the Mass of the Holy Spirit on Thursdays and the Mass of Our Lady on Saturdays. Chaplaincies were founded by fraternities and also by wealthy citizens with an eye to the welfare of their soul who gave money to create foundations so that more services could be read. New altars were built for these foundations, and in the end the old Romanesque church had twenty-five altars. However, we still know very little of the appearance of the Romanesque predecessors of the present church.

The most recent excavations (1987-1990) have revealed parts of the building including fragments of foundations which may have belonged to a relatively small church with a rectangular choir some eight metres wide. Chemical analysis of the material of which these fragments were made indicate that they can be dated to the first half of the eleventh century. The remains of a well which must have been used to supply water to the building site can be dated to the same period. A close analysis of the articles found during the excavation tells us that these are probably the remains of the chapel which was elevated to the status of a parish church in 1124. This elevation was the occasion for replacing the old place of worship with a large Roman building. At the same time a new chapter of canons was created; in return for their living they were required to perform a number of services, including extensive choir duty. The old chapel was not suited to this purpose. Some chroniclers dated the start of work on the new building in the very same year. There are some traces of building work dating back to 1132. We do not know how long the building took to complete, but there are references to a 'novum opus' [new work] in 1275.

Everything then seems to point to a replacement of the original chapel early in the twelfth century, followed by renovation as necessary at regular intervals. Archaeological remains of these periods of building work have also been found, indicating that the church was about 82 metres long and 42 metres wide with an east end in the form of a clover-leaf and a nave with three aisles. In this region a ground plan of this kind was frequently used for important churches at that time. The excavations have not supplied enough material to allow us to reconstruct this Roman place of worship. The image on the seal of the rural dean Lambertus de Rode dated 1389 may be a depiction of this church.

The construction work was not restricted to the church alone. An important event in this respect was the gift made in 1220 by the Duke of Brabant, Hendrik I, of adjoining land which increased the area owned by the church. He gave the land for the church and the canons 'ad constructionem claustri' [to build cloisters]. The chapter would be able to settle here and develop as an organized body. There are references in 1226 to a hospital dedicated to Our Lady. Pope Honorius III granted a chapel and chaplain to the monks and nuns who served the hospital. Its statutes were confirmed in 1233 and the number of livings was doubled in 1240. From this date on the chapter would have 24 canons and in 1249 they received permission to build their houses inside the 'immunitas' in return for a land tax.

Seal of the rural dean
Lambertus van Rode,
1389

The number of foundations with chaplaincies continued to grow. There were no fewer than 116 in the period from 1232 to 1547, reaching a peak in the first half of the fourteenth century. The Romanesque church was too small to accommodate them all and had to be replaced by the present building, which is the largest Gothic church in the Low Countries. An anonymous chronicle reports that work started in 1352. It was commissioned by the churchwardens, responsible for looking after the material needs of the church, who had been appointed by the Bishop of Cambrai in 1238. There were originally just two churchwardens, one layman and one priest, but the numbers were later increased. The treasurer was a canon from the chapter, assisted by churchwardens seconded from the town council who were for that reason often aldermen. They were responsible for important decisions: 'item: no expensive works should be commenced without the consent of the treasurer and the churchwardens' was the rule around 1470. Clerks were required to keep accurate accounts and oversee the labourers and the delivery of building materials. At the end of each accounting year their books were submitted for approval to the chapter and the college which comprised the burgomaster and the town sheriffs. At a meeting in the chapter's chamber the accounts were read aloud in full detail and approved.

This cooperation between the civil and spiritual authorities was quite unusual. Most collegiate churches and cathedrals were governed by the chapter, although parish churches were normally under the control of the town council. In Antwerp the chapter also held the parish rights and it was not until 1559, when most of the building work was complete, that the Church of Our Lady became a cathedral. This situation had obvious consequences for the construction work. In contrast to cathedrals, which drew their income from the entire diocese, the churchwardens only had an income from the parish topped up with grants from the city and the chapter and gifts from members of the congregation. The chapter was fully aware of the situation and was able to ensure that, in contrast to many other towns where the network of parish churches grew quite large, the Church of Our Lady remained the only full parish church in Antwerp until 1477. With very few exceptions the church received parish income from the entire city. One of the principal sources of income was derived from the obligation on Christians to receive the sacraments in the own parish and to be buried there. Although the serving chaplains, sacristans and grave diggers took some of the cake, burial fees were nevertheless a considerable source of revenue. Payment was required for the service, the use of a pall and candles, as well as a grave fee. But we should not overestimate this type of income: on the whole it represented between five and ten per cent of the church's total income. Weddings and baptisms also brought money into the church. Grants from the city were made on the grounds that, as in other cities, one of the church towers was the property of the city and the local authority looked after the chapel that served the parish. The remainder of church income came from legacies, gifts from the faithful, profits from stalls at the annual fair held within the pale, income from the church's own property and the purchase of annuities and hereditary rent-charges.

It would be hard to find a more unfortunate time to start the building work. Three years later in 1355 the Duke of Brabant, Jan III, died leaving a duchy crippled with debt. His son-in-law, the Flemish count Lodewijk van Male exercised his right to the Brabant succession and as a result Antwerp and Mechelen (Malines) were removed from the territory of Brabant and became part of Flanders. We do not know the precise effects of this situation on the course of the building work, but we can assume that it led to difficulties and delay. The next

Boss with
John the Baptist, ca. 1410

Boss with
Virgin and Child, 1993

Boss with
Saint Peter, ca. 1410

Boss with
Christ the Saviour, ca. 1440

Photo right:
Fragment of a wall painting
with the head of Christ,
first half of the 15th century

reports of construction work date from 1384 and 1385, where we find the first references to altars in the new building. Some parts were vaulted in 1391, and windows are placed in the choir in 1408. In 1406 the Antwerp magistrate gave the usual compensation for winter clothing to allow worn work on the choir to be continued; the choir vaulting was completed in 1411. This means that the late fourteenth-century and early fifteenth-century statues on corbels and the bosses in the south choir aisle are among the earliest works of art in the cathedral. The oldest examples must be dated to around 1360-1370 and are to be found in the south choir aisle. They confirm the long-held view that work on building the new church started on this site in 1352. More works of art were completed around 1400 and are found again in the choir aisle and in the chapels surrounding it. These sculptures are of great historical significance but over the course of the centuries they have been painted over so many times that a thick layer of whitewash makes it impossible to appreciate their artistic qualities today. The

restoration work carried out in 1992 on the slightly younger bosses of the sanctuary vault indicates that highly skilled stonemasons were used, although their names are not known. The first of these bosses depicts Saint John the Baptist, who can be recognized by the Lamb he carries in his arm. With his free hand he is pointing at the Lamb, reminding us of the words "See here the Lamb", spoken as he baptised Christ in the river Jordan. The next boss shows a Madonna, the mediator between heaven and earth. This is a modern sculpture which was made in 1993 to replace an original boss with an unknown subject. Then we have a relief with Saint Peter, recognizable from the key which symbolizes his ability to forgive sins. Finally, above the high altar we see Christ the Saviour. These figures owe much of their power to the fact that they were painted in bright colours. The bosses were not the only painted objects; the walls of the choir aisle and the chapels surrounding the choir aisle also had polychrome decoration. Often the primary function of this paint work was decorative, highlighting the architectural structure, but they were nevertheless of great artistic merit. There are painted borders, a considerable amount of gold leaf and even friezes of 'pressed wax brocade'. Some paintings have grown into individual works of art. At the entrance to the great sacristy a beautiful fragment of a head of Christ has been discovered under layers of whitewash. It is thought to date from the first half of the fifteenth century. The halo surrounding the head is worked in gilded stucco relief. In the next chapel, now dedicated to the Blessed Ludovicus Flores of Antwerp, we find a wall painting representing a group at Calvary and the torments of Saint Sebastian above the arms of the Bode family. The presence of these arms is a clue to the original function of the chapel, which was to enable a mass to be read in perpetuity in honour of Jan Bode, a bailiff who was murdered in 1389. The group at Calvary was probably the gift of the Guild of the Holy Cross who also used this chapel until 1492. Finally, the figure of Saint Sebastian is a reference to the Old Longbow Guild, who held their services here until 1476. A thorough restoration of the painting was completed in 1874.

The chapels in the choir aisle were being used by various guilds and chaplaincies because the rest of the Gothic church was still under construction. The foundations of the north tower were laid around 1420 under the direction of Peeter Appelmans. This immense tower made a great impression on many visitors and legends grew up around it in which even the Devil had a not inconsiderable part to play. One of these stories tells that the church was built on swampy ground and the foundations and walls kept sinking. The architect could do nothing to stop this. One of his foremen then found a mysterious old manuscript which foretold these difficulties and gave the answer. It said that the Church of Our Lady must be built on a layer of ox hides. But the foreman did not want the architect to succeed, and he concealed his discovery. He couldn't keep quiet about something so exciting, and he let his wife and children into the secret. The youngest child couldn't hold his tongue either: he told his father's secret to the architect, who tried it out and the walls shot up like magic. But that is not the end of the story. The father, seeing his evil plans frustrated, was tempted by the Devil into killing the child who had given away his secret. Soon afterwards, plagued by remorse, he fled the town and for years nothing more was heard or seen of him until one morning when the men working on the cathedral arrived to find a horribly mutilated corpse lying at the foot of the almost completed tower, dressed in pilgrim's robes. Tormented by his conscience and pursued by the Devil, the foreman had returned and thrown himself from the tower. A detail which will be of interest to tourists: in memory of this tale an ashlar memorial stone was put up at the site of the incident. According to legend, it was impossible to count the number of stones in the

Photo left:
Group at Calvary with
the torments of Saint
Sebastian and the arms of
the Bode family

mosaic covering the tombstone. There are other tales which say that it was the architect, Peeter Appelmans, who fell to his death from the tower.

Appelmans' name was mentioned in connection with the works as early as 1406, but he was certainly not the first architect of what was to become the cathedral. He succeeded James van Thienen who had been trained as a stonemason and sculptor at the Church of Our Lady of the Pool in Tienen. He worked there from 1359 or 1360 under the architect Jan van Osy whom he succeeded between 1375 and 1383. He had also worked on St. Gudule's church and the town hall in Brussels. When he took up his post in Antwerp the patrons of the building work on the Tienen church had demanded his resignation. This may be an appropriate point to look at the exact role of the architect or master builder. Who were James van Thienen, Peeter Appelmans and later on Jan Tac and Herman and Dominicus de Waghemaker and Rombout Keldermans, and especially: what exactly did they do? Some people say that they were simply skilled craftsmen who just had to keep up and follow the age-old immovable medieval traditions to build a splendid tower like that of Antwerp cathedral. The truth is that we know very little about these people and that the facts are much more complex than is often thought. Architecture changed dramatically between 1352, when the work started, and the early sixteenth century. The role of James van Thienen in the late fourteenth century and early fifteenth century was not the same as that played by Peeter Appelmans (1410-1434) or his successors Jan Tac (1434-1439), Everaert Spoorwater (1439-1474), Herman de Waghemaker (1474-1502) and his son Dominicus (1502-1542) or Rombout Keldermans (d. 1531). Like James van Thienen, Appelmans worked on a number of different important buildings simultaneously, progressing far from his stonemason origins. Church accounts preserved from the 1430s attest to his business: in 1431 Appelmans was paid 6 gr. a day while other stonemasons

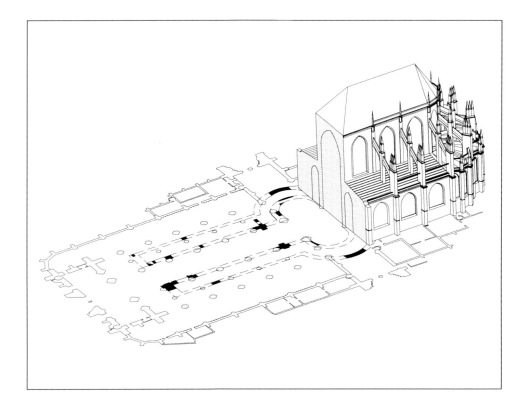

The new Gothic building around 1413

20

West front

received 5 gr. He was allocated 12 gr. a day for travelling to Brussels to buy stone. His successor Jan Tac earned 7 gr. a day and received an annual salary on top of that. Under the experienced guidance of these masters the stone stored in the building sheds was cut to templates

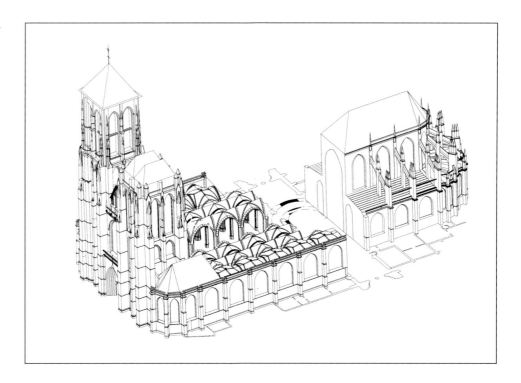

drawn by the architect and dressed by the masons. It became increasingly common to send parts of the work out to other workshops. Trade in stone grew in importance and individual masonry and sculpture workshops rose to prominence, supplying ever greater volumes of material ready for use, which meant that the building sheds became smaller. Master Everaert Spoorwater, who was the cathedral's architect between 1439 and 1474, played a significant part in this development. His buildings were at one time called 'instant churches'. Like many stonemason dynasties, the Veeweyden family, also known under the name of Spoorwater, came from Brussels. In the membership list of the stonemasons' guild of the capital of Brabant we find Coy Spoorwater in 1395, Jan Spoorwater in 1419 and Gheraart Spoorwater in 1421. In the year of his appointment in Antwerp, Everaert also took on direction of the works on the great church in Dordrecht. There too, the master builder's contract provided for payment of a fixed annual salary together with a day's wages for each day when he actually worked on the site in Dordrecht. In 1443 the master started working in Bergen-op-Zoom as well and in 1445 he was commissioned to build a new crosspiece in the Church of Saint Bavo in Haarlem. As Spoorwater had an interest in so many important works at the same time it is impossible for him to have been physically present on the site to supervise the execution of all the plans from close range. In Bergen-op-Zoom he was represented by Jan Spoorwater and in Haarlem by Hendrik Spoorwater. He seems to have considered the Antwerp commission to be the most important and did in fact move there. When he travelled abroad he was frequently referred to as 'Spoorwater van Antwerpen'. The church accounts also show that in 1456 he was present in Antwerp on no fewer than 212 of the 273 days on which the stonemasons had worked. In 1459 he was present on 248 out of 266 days and in 1465 on 197 out of 246. He visited other sites only for about ten days a year, sending the drawings and templates that the stonecutters needed from Antwerp. But although the architect was present for much of the time, it is certain that not all the stonecutting work for the Church of Our Lady was carried out in the

Antwerp building sheds. Church accounts reveal that more and more work was sent outside. Still, the Antwerp sheds did provide the successor to Master Spoorwater: Herman de Waghemaker who took over his work in Antwerp and in Hulst in 1475.

In the meantime, and in spite of a fire in 1434 which caused some damage in the choir, the building work was making good progress. The south side aisle was built between 1455 and 1469. This part of the church was needed for the Fraternity of the Holy Sacrament or Venerable, referred to above, and for the parish altar near the tower. The city council imposed a special tax on wheat for six years to finance the work. The new parish altar was consecrated in 1469 and one year later the bill for the painting of 'the third vault' was paid: this is thought to refer to the ceiling painting in the second bay. The records also tell us that in 1465 work was being carried out on Saint Arnold's chapel for the brewers' guild. We know from the depiction of brewers implements on a keystone in the northernmost side aisle, where the Saint Arnold's chapel must have been located, that work was going on there at that time. This was the real start of the seven-aisled church. Originally there was probably only a nave with three aisles, flanked by two rows laid out for chapels. In 1431 there was still talk of laying the foundations for a central aisle with double side aisles, but a ground plan drawn up in this way did not take

Ceiling painting in the second bay, probably the subject of a bill in 1470

account of the need for more new altars, needed this time for the guilds which wanted to have their own place in the church as the fraternities and chaplaincies did. Space had been agreed for bakers and millers, furriers, brewers and corn merchants, surgeons and barbers, wood-cutters, market gardeners, tailors, hosiers, coopers, linen-weavers, haberdashers, stonemasons, dealers in old clothes, painters, shoemakers, schoolmasters, joiners, smiths, carpenters, fish-mongers and mariners, innkeepers and soap-boilers. The accounts for the construction of the various pillars in the side aisles often refer to the altars to which they belonged. In 1473-1475 the churchwardens paid for pillars for the altars of Saint John (joiners), Saint Nicholas (haber-dashers) and Saint Peter and Saint Paul (bakers). The images on the keystones of the adjacent vaults indicate their position. Saint John the Evangelist, Saint Peter and Saint Paul are depicted on three consecutive bosses in the southernmost side aisle.

Work on the last few bays on the north side was not directed by Spoorwater, but was carried out in the late seventies and early eighties under Herman de Waghemaker. The old Chapel of Our Lady was demolished around 1478-1481 to make room for these bays and the transept. The new bays housed the Guild of Our Lady of Praise which was founded in 1479. One of the guild's duties was to perform an evening service of praise to the Virgin Mary every day. In order to provide a fit setting for these services the guild had its own rood loft with an organ and a platform for singers in its chapel. The service was performed by the choirmaster and four members of the chapter's choir. This chapel still contains a statue of Our Lady, the patron saint of the city. The statue that is in the chapel today dates from the late sixteenth cen-tury; it replaced an earlier statue that was destroyed when the Calvinists had control of Ant-werp (1581-1585). It is often confused with the statue of Our Lady of the Branch, a devo-tional image which was originally to be found outside the church, in the churchyard, and to which many miracles were attributed after 1475. In 1489, a record year, the money offered to

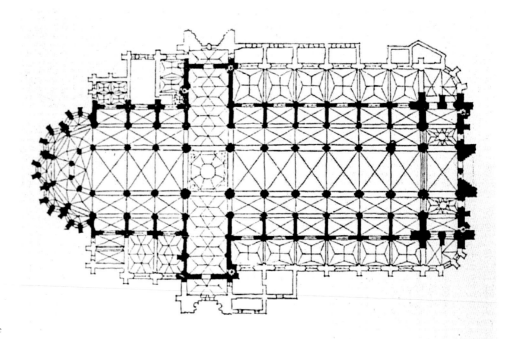

Probable ground plan of the five-aisle church

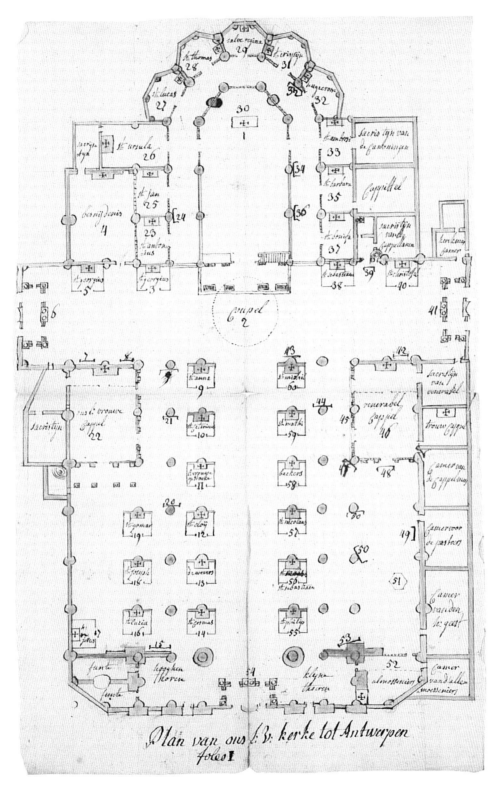

Floor plan of the church showing the position of the altars

this picture amounted to about 15% of the churchwardens' total income for the year. The sum was enough to pay 54 masons' assistants for a year.

At the same time work was continuing on both towers and the west front. The roof between the towers was covered with slate in 1471 and two years later the bill for the stone arches beneath the towers and the stone parts of the window structure was paid. The towers had already been completed as far as the belfry windows, but work on the south tower was stopped in 1475. Work continued on the fourth section of the north tower. Five years later the team moved on to the second gallery, but work on that was stopped as well. It seems that at this stage all efforts were concentrated on the transept and further work on the nave. Extending the north transept was no easy task. First of all the remaining parts of the Romanesque church had to be demolished (1482-1487) and then the churchwardens had to buy more land from the chapter because the building was going to be wider than originally planned. These problems did not arise with the construction of the south transept, which is why this part of the church was completed about twenty years earlier. At around the same time work was being done on other parts of the building, including a library, a sacristy and the Jerusalem chapel which is now dedicated to Saint Anthony. The Guild of Circumcision was to start using this chapel in 1513. It was founded in 1426 to honour the Foreskin Relic which according to legend was brought back from the Holy Land by Godfried de Bouillon and given to the city. There are references from 1325 onwards to a Circumcision Procession in which the relic was carried through the streets. The guild was an exclusive company with twenty-five members, including many sheriffs and burgomasters of the city. The relic has vanished without trace since the destruction of the images in 1566, and a picturesque tale has grown up about its disappearance. It is said that Herman Moded, a preacher and one of the main figures in the Antwerp rebellion, removed it from its reliquary during the riots and later used it to practise black magic.

In 1502 the time was thought to be ripe for the construction of the great tower. No work had been done on the tower for a quarter of a century, and new plans were needed. The architect must have been either Herman de Waghemaker or his son Dominicus who succeeded his father in the post at just that time. He also divided his time between a number of important projects. As well as the Church of Our Lady he also supervised the work on St. James' church and a new choir for St. Walburga's. In Lier he was the architect of St. Gommarus' church, in Aalst for St. Martin's and in Hulst for St. Willibrord'. He often worked with the Keldermans, a famous family of architects from Mechelen. Matthijs Kelderman was commissioned to build a row of windows in 1487 and 1489. Matthijs was particularly well-known as a stone merchant and had his own quarry in Zaventem. Under the direction his nephew Anton Keldermans work had already started on the door of the north transept. In the next few years Keldermans visited the tower several times, sometimes in the company of Alart du Hamel, another famous architect. Du Hamel had earlier supplied the design for a sacrament tower in the Venerable chapel. The visits in 1507 were probably connected with the completion of the fifth section of the great tower, which means that it had taken just five years to build.

Whoever was in fact responsible for the design, it was certainly innovative. The architect had not been content simply to continue the tower according to the earlier pattern. Above the somewhat plain architecture of the lower parts we see a section decorated with late Gothic tracery, standing on the section below and caught up between the airy arches, rising into tall pinnacles which extend the corners of the older part of the tower. This design gives the whole structure an open, airy character which is further intensified by the top section, a miracle of

Photo left:
Statue of *Our Lady*, the patron saint of Antwerp, late 16th century

Weathercock, early 16th
century, Butchers' Guild Hall
Museum, Antwerp

lace work in stone that crowns the 123 metre tower. Dominicus de Waghemaker was granted
an annuity 'because he completed the tower'. A weathercock was placed on the top as a fin-
ishing touch. The cockerel that crows to announce the day symbolizes Christ himself who
conquers dark night to bring bright day. And like a weathercock on a tower Christ turns
against the wind, against the enemies of the Church. Citizens of Antwerp have always had a
soft spot for the cockerel on the tower of their most important church. Contemporary writers
have chronicled its fortunes from the seventeenth century and still do so today. We have records of each time the gilding was renewed (1649, 1723, 1801 and 1813) and of the times
when bad weather damaged its spindle (1629). Sometimes when it had been removed for restoration, its return was accompanied by a trumpet blast from the tower; and it was not only
the craftsmen who carried out the restoration work who had their names engraved in the metal
— even the sheriffs of the city took the opportunity to have themselves commemorated in this
way as well. At least once the suggestion was made that the cock should be replaced by a gilded
hand, the symbol of Antwerp, just as Brussels had a figure of Saint Michael and Arras had a rat
on the top of their towers. The suggestion was not at all popular, especially in church circles,
even though the burgomaster suggested placing a gilded hand on top of the cock. In the nineteenth century the original cockerel was replaced by the one that is on the tower today. The
original can be seen in the Butchers' Guild Museum.

Satan has on occasions been suspected of wanting to tear down the beautiful tower.
Visitors to the great tower in the eighteenth century were shown a pair of dirty brown marks in
the stone on the second gallery and heard the tale of how the Devil had sunk his claws into the
stone at just that point with the intention of pulling the tower down. It is said that the holes

Photo right:
JEF LAMBEAUX, *Monument to*
Peeter Appelmans, 1904/1935

still stank of sulphur, but today's visitor will search in vain for those marks or for the mosaic at the foot of the tower where the unfortunate Peeter Appelmans is supposed to have met his death. It was not closely guarded and at some point it disappeared, but a bronze monument to Peeter Appelmans has been placed at the entrance to the church to replace it. The monument was originally intended for Jan Appelmans, Peeter's father, who was thought in the nineteenth century to have been the first architect of the church. There is however no evidence to support this view, and it is not even entirely clear that Jan Appelmans was Peeter's father, nor that he was an architect. But Peeter Appelmans certainly did play an important part in the construction of the tower in the early fifteenth century. The monument in his honour was given to the city by the former sheriff Van den Nest in 1904 and was made by the sculptor Jef Lambeaux. It was not until 1935 that the statue was placed in its present position by the front of the church.

It was now no longer necessary to complete the second tower. Dominicus de Waghemaker and Rombout Keldermans had received a commission to design a new and larger choir. The new choir along with the crypt, double choir aisle and nine radiating chapels would mean a much larger church than the existing one. The central aisle would become a side aisle and the south side aisles would have to be removed to make way for a new central aisle on the same level as the small tower, which would itself be replaced by a new high portal. The original plans had provided for a third tower above the crossing between the nave and the transept, but this tower had not yet been built and was no longer needed in the original place. In 1497-98 work was still being done on the octagon above the crossing pillars. Much of the stonework was supplied by Hendrik van Pede, the Brussels city architect.

The new plans were not just left on paper. Emperor Charles laid the first stone on the 15th of July 1521. If we are to believe the verses written by Godefridus Bouvaert, he also took the opportunity of visiting the great tower which had just been completed, and was inspired to make a speech in its honour:

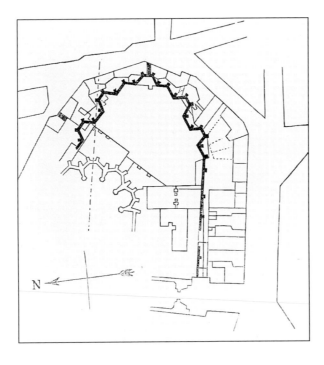

Reconstruction of the ground plan of the choir according to the 1521 plans for expansion of the church

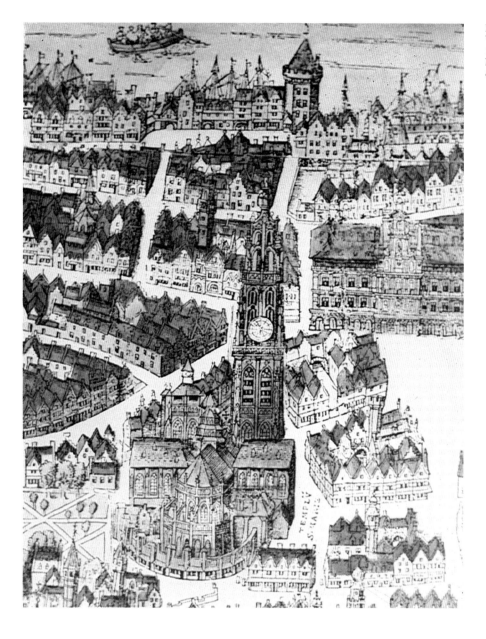

Map of Antwerp by
VERGILIUS BONONIENSIS,
1565, detail with small
houses built up against the
choir

Beloved city of the arts, favoured above countless others!
In all my realms there is no other tower to equal it;
The tower in Strasbourg is not so lovely
Though it climbs as high, or just a little higher.
Its fame has spread all over Europe.
I wish there were a cash till inside this gem
And if the people who have come from far and wide
Could see it only once a year,
I would not be afraid to spend my gold
To gild the tower if I could;
And still it would be too little and gold too mean a substance,

Its beauty deserves much more and demands a greater praise.
Antwerp, come what may, preserve this jewel,
That was six and ninety years in the making.
Your other monuments may fall, but do not be concerned,
The city will be famous as long as the tower stands.

It is probable that part of the reason for these highly ambitious plans were the glowing eco-nomic prospects for the city and its trade. The population had grown to about 60,000, double the figure around 1480. Antwerp was one of the largest cities north of the Alps. It had become the centre of world trade, and the wind of good fortune wafted over church wardens as well. Church income had never been higher. Much of this income was derived from hiring out stalls on the old church lands during the annual fairs and stands in the Onze-Lieve-Vrouwepand, a covered market that the churchwardens had decided to build in 1460 for artists, sculptors, joiners and book dealers. It lay to the south of the churchyard. More and more buildings were being put up on church lands, including shops and houses that were rented out to raise funds for the church. The church also sold the right to let the land for rent. Income from these sources was the most important contribution made by the chapter, which owned the land, to the construction of the church. When the new choir was built, small structures that could be used as shops and houses were built against the choir walls; they were rented out to raise funds to keep the site working. The churchwardens took their task to heart and within a few years several columns and a substantial part of the choir wall had been completed. But in the mean-time other religious groups had noticed the city's growing prosperity and wanted their share of the gifts made by the congregation. In around 1517 the Dominicans started to build a new church near their monastery. Work was continuing on St. James' church. The Augustines were building what was to become St. Andrew's, and a new choir was built for St. Walburga's. In addition to all this activity, one day after the first stone was laid, books by Luther were burnt in public for the first time in Antwerp. One of the practices condemned by Luther was the sale of indulgences, a custom which had brought in so much money for building the church. You can imagine the consequences: after just a few years the construction fever abated. The amount of work that had been done can be seen from a view of the city dated 1565 and from excava-tions which took place around 1850 in the garden of the adjoining deanery.

Although income had fallen, the new project was not simply allowed to wither away. The end came suddenly and unexpectedly. A fierce fire broke out in 1533. A candle that had not been properly extinguished set fire to the St. Gommarus altar by the north tower and the fire spread to the wooden truss above the central aisle and the transept, where the vault had not yet been completed. The truss fell burning to the ground where it remained smouldering for several days. The damage was enormous: not only to the building itself but also to the furnishings which had been supplied by the guilds, companies and fraternities. As a result of this disaster and other circumstances only two of the sixty or so altarpieces which were in the church at the time have been preserved. The first is a triptych commissioned by the joiners' guild in 1508 from Quentin Metsys depicting *God's distress (Christ in tears)*, with *Salomé with the head of John the Baptist* and the *Torment of John the Evangelist* on the side panels. The panel exteriors show John the Baptist and John the Evangelist again as the patron saints of the joiners' guild. This triptych is now displayed in the Royal Museum of Fine Art where it is one of the high points of the collection. Another triptych now housed in the same museum is *The Last Judgement* and the *Works of Charity* by the Brussels artist Barend van Orley which was painted in 1519 for the almoners' chapel. Before the fire in 1533 these kinds of paintings were still the exception to the rule. Most of the altars in the church had sculpted reredos, a form of art in which sculptors from Antwerp had earned renown abroad. For example, Gillis Wraghe made a wooden reredos for the Guild of Our Lady of Praise in 1501. Gillis van der Sluys was commissioned to produce a similar object for the Guild of Saint Luke in 1499 to be installed in the chapel of his own guild, and he also received a commission from the guild of dealers in old clothes. The citizens of Antwerp were also not above granting commissions on several occasions to outside masters in preference to people from their own city. Relations with artists from Brussels in particular were excellent, and artists based in Antwerp gave permission for their colleagues from Brussels to use the building of Onze-Lieve-Vrouw to sell their wares. The Guild of Saint Luke, to which Antwerp artists belonged, gave a commission to Colin 'van Bruesele' (Colijn de Coter) to paint the walls of its chapel in the choir

UNKNOWN ARTIST, *The fire in Antwerp cathedral in 1533*, Bachte-Maria-Leerne, Ooidonk Palace

aisle. Even the Gothic pulpit, which was originally going to be made by a local craftsman, was in the end supplied from Brussels. This article can still be seen on some seventeenth-century drawings of the church interior. It was eventually sold and removed from the church during the French Revolution.

Along with reredos and a pulpit there were many other works of art in the church, including stained glass windows. Window embrasures had been put into position as long ago as 1391 and 1408, when the Gothic choir was under construction. The first window was the

Barend van Orley,
The Last Judgement, Antwerp,
Royal Museum of Fine Art,
1519

gift of a knight, Willem van Berchem. The other was put up when three burghers were ordered by the bailiff to pay for a window depicting Saint Peter and Saint Paul, the patron saints of the first church in Antwerp. Spanish merchants paid for a window in 1481-1482. Very few of these treasures have been preserved, with the exception of a glass window of John the Baptist and John the Evangelist from around 1520-1525 that has been restored and is still in the church.

The fire had caused tremendous damage and the plans for the 'new church' were

shelved for a while. All available resources were used to make sure that the normal routine of the church could continue. Work on repairing the damage started immediately. Large quantities of wood, slate and glass were bought and a few months later the maypole appeared on the dome of the crossing. The truss was replaced and the stone cladding on the columns in the central aisle which had broken up in the great heat was given a plaster coat. We know nothing about the final vaulting of the central aisle and the transept. It was in fact the absence of a vault which had allowed the fire to cause so much damage. The reason is clear: the plans for a new church had not yet been completely abandoned. Two years after the fire Lodewijk van Boghem, an architect attached to the duke's court, and Hendrik van Pede, the city architect of Brussels, were paid a fee for inspecting three designs for the new choir. Two of them had been drafted by Philips Lammekens, who became the architect in charge of the Church of Our Lady in 1543, and the third was the work of Cornelis Yman, Mechelen city architect, and Thomas Zammele. This time the plans stayed on the drawing board.

Work was progressing well on restoration of the building. Anton and Johann Jakob Fugger donated a new stained glass window depicting *The conversion and the mission of Saint Paul* (1537) in front of the central aisle where it remains to this day. The Abbey of St. Bavo in Ghent, the Park Abbey in Heverlee, the Abbey of St. Bernard in Hemiksem and the Abbey of St. Trond each gave a window. Burgomaster Dassa and his wife Barbara Rockox donated the glass window representing the *Adoration of the Kings*. The guilds helped to restore their own altars. Around 1550 Hans van Elburgh painted a triptych for the fishmongers guild. The cen-

HANS VAN ELBURGH,
The miracle of the fishes, centre
panel, 1589

tre panel and some parts of the predella are still kept in the church. Frans Floris painted the
Fall of the Rebellious Angels for the swordsmen's guild in 1554. The painting is now in the Royal
Museum of Fine Art. By 1555 work had progressed so far that the Order of the Golden Fleece
could meet in the Church of Our Lady. A new High Altar was built for this occasion and Philip II donated the three windows above it, which have been preserved to this day.

Violencias y Sacrilegios que los Herejes usaron contra las Imagines de Christo y de los Santos en la Yglesia Cathedral de Amberez.

From the destruction of the images to the Fall of Antwerp

T he city on the Scheldt was not long to enjoy the fruits of the great efforts it had made to restore its principal church to its former glory. Lutherism was followed by the more militant Calvinism. In contrast to Lutherans and Anabaptists who respected civic authority, Calvin taught his followers that they must follow the law of God in preference to the law of Man. Calvinists also held that 'there should be no statues and images of saints in the church and that they should be eradicated; the Martinists (followers of Luther) did not want to be so fanatical and cause aggravation, but suggested leaving them as stones or blocks but not decorate them or place lights before them, or honour or venerate them'. That is how Godevaert van Haecht described the situation in his chronicle of the events. The reformists were indeed strongly opposed to the worship of images, seeing it as a kind of idolatry and pointing to the prohibition on images contained in the Old Testament. In Roman Catholic theology however, the veneration of images was permissible and useful provided that the image was not honoured in itself or for its own qualities, but only as the representation of God, Christ or a saint. This view had been confirmed by the important Council of Trent in 1563. Protestant convictions had already led to a destruction of images in other towns: starting in Wittenberg (1522) and spreading to Zürich (1523), Copenhagen (1530), Münster (1534), Geneva (1535) and Augsburg (1537). The first case in the Low Countries happened on the 10th of August 1566 in Steenvoorde, just south of what is today the border between France and Belgium. It was feared that the trend could spread to Antwerp. On the 18th of August a traditional procession was normally held to celebrate the Feast of the Assumption of the Virgin Mary, during which the image of the Madonna was taken out of the cathedral and carried around the city. In other years there had been more than enough volunteers to carry the statue. The fact that this year people had to be paid to do it was an ominous sign. Rumour had it that bets had been laid on whether the statue would return to the cathedral safe and sound after the

GASPARD BOUTTATS, *The destruction of the images, 1566,* etching, Antwerp, City Print Collection, 17th century strange speeches that Calvinist preachers had made on the cult of images. William of Orange was in the city and postponed his departure until after the procession, convinced that his presence would deter any agitators. The statue survived undamaged, but some of the crowd had not behaved respectfully. Insults were shouted. The clergy therefore decided to put the image back behind lock and key immediately instead of displaying it in the centre of the church for eight days, as had been the custom. On the following day the preacher Herman Moded once again called on his followers to cast down images. After a disturbance in the cathedral a number of agitators were locked in and started to sing psalms. A crowd gathered and forced its way inside, and then started to smash the images: 'there were hardly enough big smiths' hammers and axes of all sorts as they were used to open all the rooms and closets with such violence that nothing in the church remained whole except when some of the leaders of the guilds managed to make their way through the crowd and protect their altars with entreaties, or take them to pieces and carry them away. At the time it looked as if this had been a spontaneous uprising, but afterwards it appeared to have been planned. Some of the agitators had bought axes a few days beforehand, and others had hired people to help with the destruction, paying them varying amounts according to their physical strength. Once the images in the cathedral had been destroyed, the iconoclasts split up into smaller groups and moved on to the other churches and monasteries in the city. When they had finished with Antwerp they moved on to 's-Hertogenbosch, Bergen-op-Zoom, Lier and Turnhout. It took days to clear away the rubble, and on the 23rd of August some of the iconoclasts started 'to smash down some thick walls of the private choirs, to make the church plain'.

Peace returned relatively quickly and the magistrate was able to order the guilds to restore their altars on the 9th of September. The accounts of a number of guilds confirm that debris and rubble had to be cleared away before restoration work could start. It was to take a long time. Some guilds complained that they did not have enough money to restore their altar to its previous splendour. A new altar was put up for the innkeepers' guild in 1568 and in the same year Willem Key painted a new picture entitled *Repentant Sinners* for the haberdashers. Canon du Terne donated an *Adoration of the Shepherds* by Frans Floris for the horticulturalists' altar. Crispyn van den Broeck made a new altarpiece for the Young Longbow guild and Maarten de Vos painted a *Doubting Thomas* for the altar of the furriers' guild and a *Saint George with the Dragon* for the fencers' guild.

Most of these paintings are no longer in the church; the cathedral's history was far too turbulent. Shortly after the destruction of the images Spain and the Low Countries became caught up in the Eighty Years' War. One of the causes for this war was the dissatisfaction felt by the nobility with the way that Philip II allowed the Low Countries to be governed from Spain by officials in Brussels. The destruction of the images had split the population into two camps: those who remained faithful to the Church of Rome and accepted the authority of the governors; and committed Calvinists and discontented noblemen who turned against Philip II to line up behind William of Orange. The Duke of Alba was sent by the king to restore order but simply provoked further discontent with his Council of Troubles, new taxes, use of the inquisition and his decision to send garrisons to the towns. The 'Spanish Fury' raged through Antwerp from the fourth to the seventh of November. After the capture of Zierikzee from the rebels, poorly paid Spanish soldiers rose in mutiny. At the end of October the rebels gathered in Antwerp and ransacked the city. Robbery, murder and fire plagued the city. One of the buildings that suffered the worst damage was the new Renaissance town hall. The cathedral

Photo right:
HENDRIK I VAN STEENWIJCK, *Cathedral interior*, 1583 or 1594, Budapest, Szépmüvézeti Museum

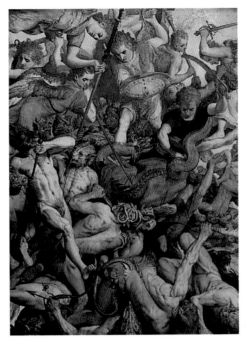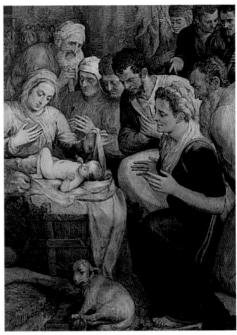

was miraculously spared but remained closed for a few days as a precaution. The Fury speeded up the Pacification of Ghent which in turn led to the withdrawal of the Spanish troops. Two years later the city came under Calvinist control and the magistrate appointed Calvanist deans to head the guilds. Before long the six companies that had the right to bear arms and the other guilds asked for permission to remove their altars from the church. Celebration of Catholic services was forbidden and the church was cleansed of 'Papist' furnishings, as it was to be reconsecrated as a Calvinist place of worship. 'Communion' was celebrated in the choir of the cathedral on the 19th of November 1581. Antwerp was to remain under Calvinist control for four years, ending with the capture of the city by Alexander Farnese on the 17th of August 1585. But after this date the Scheldt remained closed, trade was down and the city's decline continued. Only 50,000 inhabitants were left of the 90,000 who had lived in Antwerp at the end of the Calvinist period. About twenty thousand people left in the first ten months after the city had been taken by Farnese and peace had been restored: many of those who left were prosperous citizens. Around the middle of the sixteenth century there had been more than 1,500 merchants involved in international trade living in Antwerp, but by 1625 there were only around five hundred. In spite of this Antwerp was still an important economic centre, specializing in the manufacture of luxury goods such as furniture, statuary and especially paintings. Rubens, Jordaens, Van Dyck and the other artists in their circle were to bring lasting fame to the Antwerp School. They had the chance to display their talents when the churches were restored after the second, or 'silent' destruction of the images when the city was under Calvinist control.

Reconstruction after 1585

Just a few weeks after Farnese had conquered Antwerp for Spain the guilds were ordered to rebuild their altars in the church. Some pleaded poverty (or was it caution?) and put back the old altars that had been removed from the church five years before. Most of these altars dated from after the first destruction of the images and were not yet twenty years old. Still, some of the guilds decided to commission new works, and the reasons are easy to see. In the aftermath of the Council of Trent (1545-1563) had come the Counter-Reformation, a triumphalist movement aimed at a fundamental reshaping of the old beliefs that on occasions took an exalted and militant position in defending the Roman church against Protestantism. The Guild of Saint Ambrose, the patron saint of schoolmasters, joined forces with the soap-boilers to commission an altarpiece from Frans Francken. The central tableau shows *Jesus at the age of twelve among the scribes* (Luke 2: 41-50). Some of the scribes are thought to represent Luther, Calvin and Melanchton. This indicates that the panel can be interpreted as an attack on the reformers, who are being shown the truth by Christ himself.

FRANS FRANCKEN THE ELDER, *Jesus at the age of twelve among the scribes,* centre panel of the altarpiece of the Schoolmasters' Guild, 1587

The side panels show the *Baptism by Ambrose of Saint Augustine, patron saint of schoolmasters,* and *The prophet Elijah with the widow of Sarepta.*

One of the most sought-after painters of altarpieces was Maarten de Vos, despite the fact that he had held Lutheran views. He painted a triptych of *Christ after the Resurrection* for the Old Arbalest Guild. His *Temptation of Saint Anthony* adorned the altar of the companies of Saint Anthony and Saint Hubert. For the Guild of Saint Luke he painted a masterly *Saint Luke with the Madonna.* All these altarpieces are now housed in the Royal Museum of Fine Art. The only one of his works to remain in the cathedral is the centre panel of his altarpiece for the innkeepers' guild. Appropriately it depicts *The marriage in Cana* where Christ turned water into wine. This panel shows a marked Venetian influence, which is not surprising since De Vos spent some time in the City of the Doges and knew the Venetian school very well.

Altars were not the only parts of the church to be decorated with paintings; triptychs depicting appropriate themes were also commissioned for epitaphs and memorial stones. One

example of such work is the *Last Judgement* painted by Jacob de Backer for the epitaph of the famous printer Christopher Plantin. As was customary the client had portraits of himself with his wife and children painted on the side panels.

No significant renovation work was done on the church interior until the seventeenth century. The Twelve Year Truce started in 1609 and was a welcome break for the Low Countries in the Eighty Year War and also signified a de facto recognition of the split between the Low Countries and the Protestant Republic of the United Provinces. The south of the country remained Catholic and under Spanish rule. The River Scheldt was still closed. A Te Deum was held in the cathedral to celebrate the declaration of the truce and one of the specially created decorations was a chronogram: 'goD Moet nU enDe aLtijt geLoeft sijn', meaning: praise god now and always.

And how better to praise Him during the Counter-Reformation than by refurbishing His house? A decree ordering the restoration of the churches was made by Archdukes Albrecht and Isabella on the 28th of March 1611. The Antwerp city magistrate decided that collections would be made during the High Mass and the sermons to raise funds for church restoration. As far as the cathedral was concerned it was not simply a question of repairing damage. The civil unrest of earlier years had not just prevented 'new work' being carried out. As the plans had called for expansion of the building, the church that had been started in 1352 was still not complete. The nave and the transepts were still bridged in wood. The churchwardens had never managed to have the stone vaulting put in place. Some of the doors and facades were not finished. Considerable financial support was provided by the archducal couple, followed by the city council and individual donors. The first stone of the nave vault was laid on the 20th of July 1613. It was agreed that the work would follow the pattern of the two-hundred-year-old sanctuary vault. The six bosses bear the coats of arms of, from east to west, the Duchy of Brabant, the Shire of Antwerp, the City of Antwerp, the Infanta Isabella, the Archduke Albrecht and the chapter of the cathedral. After this work was complete, the north transept was vaulted, the front of the church was finished and part of the adjoining Chapel of the Circumcision was vaulted. Once again the work was supported by gifts from Albrecht and Isabella and the city magistrate. The high point was the splendid stained glass window in the facade of the north transept representing Albrecht and Isabella kneeling before Christ on the cross. Finally the other transept was completed and a new stained glass window was put in place. It shows the Virgin Mary surrounded by angels above the figure of King Philip III kneeling before a crucifix. Albrecht and Isabella paid for the window in the north transept and the king paid for the one in the south transept. The window depicting Philip III has not survived. These two stained glass windows were not the only decorative articles placed in the church at this time; they were part of a broader iconographic programme which included four more windows in the north transept. The first represented Godfried de Bouillon accompanied by the Antwerp chapter and twelve knights. This alluded to the legend that the chapter had been founded by the Duke and was paid for by some of the canons. The second window depicts the *Veneration of Our Lady of the Branch* and parts of this window have been preserved. The Brotherhood of the Circumcision paid for a window showing the *Circumcision of Christ* and the fourth window is a memorial to Dean Johannes del Rio kneeling before the cross.

Next page:
J. CUSSERS, Stained glass window with *Albrecht and Isabella*, 1616

The role of Peter Paul Rubens in the renovation of reredos paintings cannot be underestimated. After his first apprenticeship with Tobias Verhaecht, with whom he probably studied because of family ties, he spent four years perfecting his skills under Adam van Noort and then moved to the workshop of Otto van Veen, one of the most prominent artists in Antwerp and a member of the 'Romanist' circle: a group of artists who had made the usual study tour of Italy and were strongly influenced by Humanism and the

PETER PAUL RUBENS, *The Assumption of the Virgin Mary,* 1625-1626

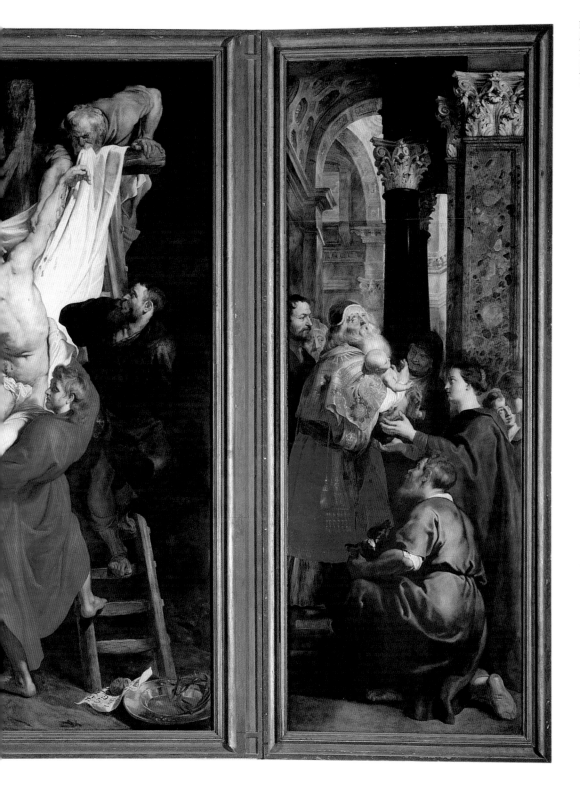

PETER PAUL RUBENS, *The Descent from the Cross,* with *The Presentation in the Temple* and *The visit of Mary to her niece Elisabeth,* on the side panels, 1612

Renaissance. Rubens was himself admitted as a master to the Guild of Saint Luke in 1598. He stayed with Van Veen for two years, probably waiting to leave for Italy. There are two works by Van Veen in the cathedral today: a small panel with a representation of the *Raising of Lazarus* and a large *Last Supper* on canvas. The latter piece was probably painted for the Venerable altar in 1610. In 1608 Rubens returned from Italy on hearing that his mother was seriously ill. By the time he arrived in Antwerp she had already died, and Rubens was probably nursing plans of a return to Italy, where he had already built up a solid reputation. He had been working in the service of the Duke of Mantua and had painted altarpieces for churches in Rome, Fermo and Genua. A glittering career awaited him in Italy. Albrecht and Isabella offered him the position of court artist and Rubens accepted on condition that he could settle in Antwerp rather than living at court in Brussels. He must have realized that he would have the chance to work on many prestigious projects in Antwerp and that his Italian reputation had preceded him.

Almost as soon as he had returned to Antwerp Rubens received important commissions for the State Chamber in the town hall, for St. Paul's church, St. Walburga's church and especially for the cathedral. His first order for the cathedral came from the Civil Guard or harquebusiers' guild and was for a painting for their altar in the south transept of the church. The Civil Guard were the youngest of the six city companies that had the right to bear arms. Their members were not soldiers but citizens who purchased a set of arms to help defend the city in times of crisis, in return for which they received a number of privileges. They met in the Guild Chamber in the presence of their dean, burgomaster Nicolas Rockox, to decide who should receive the commission. Rubens was probably chosen partly as a result of the support of Rockox, who was not only the dean of the Civil Guard and burgomaster but also a 'friend and patron' of Rubens, who had also recently bought a house on the Wapper, making him a rear neighbour of the guild. The choice of the theme for the painting cannot have been easy. The patron saint of the guild was Saint Christopher, but it was not possible to choose an episode from the life of St. Christopher. Following the decisions of the Council of Trent, the third diocesan synod of the diocese of Antwerp had insisted that the chapter must ensure that at least the centre panels of triptychs contained a figure of Christ or a scene from the New Testament. The aim was to stop unreliable legends about the saints being popularized through paintings in churches. This was one subject on which the Catholic and Protestant authorities agreed. The legend of Saint Christopher was a case in point: both Erasmus and Luther had pointed out that the tale of Christopher certainly contained a fine moral, but the saint had never existed. Christopher was a giant who was said to have carried the Christ child across a stream. He was originally known as Reprobus and only later called Christopher, a name that is derived from the Greek and literally means 'bearer of Christ'. Christopher carried the Child over the stream on his shoulders and bore Him in his body through chastisement, in his mind through his innermost thoughts and in his mouth through confession of faith and preaching. Historians soon noted that the three panels of the triptych painted by Rubens each represent bearers of Christ. On the left we see the Virgin Mary visiting her niece Elisabeth. She is with child, and so is bearing Christ. Christ is also borne in the centre panel, the *Descent from the Cross*. All the figures by the cross are in some way bearing the body of the crucified figure. On the right-hand panel Rubens has painted Simeon in the temple. The old priest Simeon, to whom God had made a promise that he would see the Saviour before his death, is holding the Child in his arms, and so is another 'bearer of Christ'. The man seen in profile behind Simeon is thought to be Nicolaas Rockox, the dean of the guild. Christopher himself does in fact appear on the

outer sides of the panels. Rubens used a sketch he had made in Italy after an ancient image of Hercules for the muscular figure of the giant. There is a symbolic double meaning here as well: just as the world weighed so heavily on Hercules' shoulders, so did the Christ child weigh on the shoulders of Christopher because he was bearing 'not only the whole world... but also Him who made the world'. Next to Christopher we see a hermit with a lamp that, according to mediaeval legend, lit Christopher's path in the darkness. The hermit also showed Christopher the path by teaching him to believe, and Christ is the lamp that lightens the darkness for

PETER PAUL RUBENS,
The Resurrection of Christ,
centre panel of the epitaph
to Jan Moretus, 1612

Christians. The lamp in the hands of the hermit is therefore Christ, and the hermit is also a bearer of Christ.

Although some writers and theologians of the Counter-Reformation had expressed aversion to mediaeval devotional writings and legends, they remained an important influence on church art. This influence can be seen in the *Assumption of the Virgin Mary* that Rubens painted for the main altar of the cathedral. Tradition has it that after the ascension of Christ, Mary lived in seclusion until an angel appeared to her to announce her death. The apostles, who had been travelling all over the world to spread the faith, were miraculously returned to the Holy Land and were present at her death, after which they took the body to the grave and kept watch over it. Three days later they witnessed the Madonna's assumption to heaven in the company of angels. The picture was not completed without difficulties. In September 1611 Otto van Veen, Rubens' master during his apprenticeship, submitted a design for a *Coronation of the Virgin Mary* to the church council; this subject is liturgically very close to the Assumption. One month later Rubens put forward two designs: one with the Coronation of the Virgin Mary and one with the Assumption. The client chose the Assumption, but the panel was never put in its intended place, being sent instead to the Houtappel Chapel in the Jesuit church of Antwerp. It was thought in the eighteenth century that the painting had been found too small for the cathedral and that the authorities had decided to dispose of it. The panel is now in the Vienna Kunsthistorisches Museum. There was no further talk of a new painting for the high altar until 1618 when Rubens submitted two designs and the De Nole brothers made a stone model of the altar in which the work was to be placed. In the meantime the chapter was trying

PETER PAUL RUBENS,
Two angels, outer panels of the
epitaph to Jan Moretus,
1612

to find the necessary funds and made an agreement with dean Del Rio that he would bear the cost of the altarpiece in return for the right to be buried in the church. In 1621 the De Nole brothers, sculptors, signed a contract stipulating that the work must be completed before Easter 1624. Rubens could not be hurried. His busy life, his travels on diplomatic business, other important commissions and the outbreak of plague in Antwerp meant that he had only limited time to devote to this piece. In 1626 he asked for the choir of the church to be cleared so that he could work undisturbed. This request was granted. When the panel was brought to the church it was clear that the dimensions of the painting did not fit the space left for it in the altar, so it had to be taken back to the workshop for adjustment. It was finally set in its place in May that year.

In spite of the difficulties referred to above, Rubens still found time to create triptychs for some prominent citizens who wanted to be commemorated in the cathedral. Two of these have survived. The triptych for Jan Michielsen and Maria Maes is now in the Antwerp Royal Museum of Fine Art and depicts *Christ in the Hay*. The church has a nineteenth-century copy of the centre panel in the epitaph to Arnolf-François de Pret and Marie-Petronille Moretus. The Moretus triptych, made for the epitaph to Jan Moretus and Martina Plantin, is still in the cathedral, in the chapel of Our Lady of Peace. The subject chosen by the client was an appropriate one: the *Resurrection of Christ*. To the left we find *John the Baptist*, the patron saint of Jan Moretus, and on the right is *Saint Martina*, his wife's patron saint. John can be recognized by his camelhair cloak and Martina carries the palm that alludes to her martyrdom. Her posture and the way her robe is draped are reminiscent of a late-Hellenic image of Ceres. The falling pillars and the image of Apollo in the background refer to the legend according to which Martina refused to obey the emperor's command that she should make an offering to Apollo, whose temple was destroyed when she made the sign of the cross. The Christ figure on the centre panel is similar in composition to that of the high priest in the well-known Laocoon group of great antiquity. When Rubens was in Italy he made sketches of this statue and of the Hercules figure from the collection of the Farnese family. The influence of ancient Rome on Rubens' work can be seen most clearly on the reverse sides of the panels. When the triptych is closed we see two angels each holding one of the rings of a great door, ready to open it. Rubens was familiar with the composition of a first-century Roman memorial altar which he had the opportunity to study during his time in Rome. On that piece, two winged Victories open the gates to the underworld. In Rubens' Christian version the angels remind us of the angels seen at Christ's grave on the morning of the resurrection. The figure on the left is a direct reference to the ancient Flora Farnese, another sculpture copied by the master during his time in Rome. He also painted an epitaph with a *Madonna and Child* for the Goubau family. It is now in the Musée des Beaux-Arts in Tours.

HENDRIK VAN BALEN,
John the Baptist before Herod and
Mary with the angels, side panels
of the altarpiece made for
the joiners' guild, 1622

Peter Paul Rubens was by no means the only artist to receive prestigious commissions for the cathedral. The joiners' guild had sold its famous triptych by Quentin Metsys to the city and had a replacement painted by Hendrik van Balen. The subject is *John the Baptist preaching* and the panels are still in the cathedral. The same artist also painted a triptych for the epitaph to the merchant Filip Heemsen and his wife Anna van Eelen. Only the centre panel of this work, a representation of the *Holy Family*, has been kept in the church. Frans Francken the Elder painted a new picture for the masons and in 1640 Anthony van Dyck received a commission from the Young Archers' Guild, but the work was never done. To replace this missing work a competition was arranged between Cornelis Schut and Thomas Willeboirts Bosschaert: each of them would submit a painting and the guild would buy the better one. Cornelis Schut carried off the prize and was also commissioned to provide a circular painting on canvas for the crossing tower. The chosen theme was the same as that of the painting above the high altar: the *Assumption of the Virgin Mary*.

It would take far to long to describe all the paintings which were created for the cathedral in the first half of the seventeenth century. As for carvers and sculptors, it would seem they contributed little to this stage of the church's development.

Nevertheless, the carvers and sculptors of Antwerp were just as active as the painters. Examples of their work include the architectural framework for the new altarpieces for the church. The work of the De Nole brothers on the high altar of the cathedral has already been

Hendrik van Balen,
Holy Family, ca. 1622

mentioned. The new liturgical rules following the Council of Trent had meant a great many orders for carvers and sculptors. Sermons attacking Protestant dogma took on a more important role in the counter-reformation offensive under the influence of the Jesuits in particular and were a factor in the trend towards exuberant styles of pulpit design. Confessionals and communion rails also reflected the new rules, emphasizing the attachment of the Catholic Church to the old doctrine of the sacraments, especially confession and the Eucharist, which were questioned by the Protestant faith. Most of these articles of furniture were also used for private devotions which were more common in the cloister churches such as those of the Dominicans or Jesuits. Examples of this style are to be found in St. Paul's church and in the Church of St. Charles Borromeo, both of which were among the first to install highly ornate baroque pulpits. The cathedral kept the old Gothic pulpit until the French Revolution. The confessionals which are now in the cathedral date from the nineteenth century. A considerable amount of important sculptural work was done in the Church of Our Lady in the early seventeenth century. Three enclosed porches decorated with monumental images were erected. The outer porch on the west front acquired a statue of the Virgin, and a carving of the Last Judgement was added to the arch above the great doors. An enclosed porch was built inside the

CORNELIS SCHUT, *The Assumption of the Virgin Mary,* 1647

Confessional, detail,
attributed to WILLEM
KERRICX

Attributed to JOOS DE
CORT, Fragment of a statue
from the southern enclosed
porch

church next to these doors. It was made of different kinds of marble and alabaster and was partly paid for by Bishop Malderus. About twenty years later similar enclosed porches were built for the north and south transepts. Two figures in white marble that are now in a yard next to the church may have been taken from the south porch. More significant was the row of apostle figures that were erected against the pillars in the nave and served as epitaphs. They can still be seen on some paintings of the church interior. Work probably started on these figures soon after the nave was vaulted. Records from the archives show that the chapter sometimes gave permission for an epitaph if the applicant agreed to pay for one of the figures. An inscribed cartouche then completed the epitaph. The church also housed memorials to the bishops of Antwerp. Franciscus Sonnius (d. 1576) and Laevinus Torrentius (d. 1595) were followed in 1613 by Johannes Miraeus (d. 1611), whose memorial was sculpted by the De Nole brothers, and Johannes Malderus (d. 1633), commemorated by Hans van Mildert. However, these important works of art did not survive the French Revolution and the only monument to their successors that has been preserved is that of Bishop Capello (d. 1676). This is a piece by Artus Quellin the Elder, a member of a famous Antwerp dynasty of sculptors whose renown spread as far as Scandinavia in the seventeenth and early eighteenth centuries. There is another monument to Bishop Capello; this one was made by Hendrik Frans Verbrugghen in the same year and is still to be found at the rear of the church on the former site of the almoners' altar.

It was erected by the almoners in thanks to Bishop Ambrosius Capello, a Dominican from a prosperous Italian family, who had given a large part of his wealth to the almoners for the poor.

ARTUS QUELLIN THE ELDER, *Memorial to Bishop Ambrosius Capello*, detail, 1676

D·O·M·
F. MARIVS AMBROSIVS
CAPELLO
Ex Denominato Yprensi
VII. Episcopus Antverpiæ
ibidem natus A 1597
Elect: Præ[...]. Pont: [...]us A 10[...]
Obijt [...] 16[...]

Ill:mo ac Reu:Dno
F. AMBROSIO CAPELLO
ord: Prædicatorum
VII ANTVERP. EPISCOPO
in vita et in morte
ARCHI-ELEEMOSYNARIO
(dixi satis)
ELEEMOSYNARII ex asse hæredes
hoc et grato animo P.P.
MDCLXXVI

Hendrik Frans Verbrugghen, *Epitaph to Bishop Ambrosius Capello*, 1676

Photo left:
Artus Quellin the
Elder, *Memorial for Bishop
Ambrosius Capello*, 1676

These two works of art bring us into the second half of the seventeenth century, a period when more attention was given to sculpture than to painting. The marble used in the porch altars was no longer simply a surround for a painted triptych; it was the architectural framework and a work of sculptural art in its own right. Sculptors such as Artus Quellin the Elder, already referred to above, Hendrik Frans Verbrugghen and Lodewijk Willemsens came to prominence. Quellin collaborated with Huybrecht van den Eynde on a marble altar for the swordsmens' guild. The life-size statues of Joshua and Gideon attest to the skills of these men. The churchwardens' chamber of the cathedral houses a marble relief from the predella of the hosiers' altar made by Peter Verbrugghen II. Two marble medallions depicting Saint Eligius and Saint Walburga probably come from the altar which Hendrik Frans Verbrugghen and Artus Quellin the Elder made for the smiths' guild. Fragments of the coopers' altar, another piece made by Quellin and Lodewijk Willemsens in 1677-1678, are now in the high altar. They are among the most beautiful works of sculpture made in that period in Europe. A marble enclosure made by Willem Kerricx was placed around the original altar about five years later. Two fragments of that sculpture are still in the church. Artus Quellin the Elder and Peter

ARTUS QUELLIN THE
ELDER and LODEWIJK
WILLEMSENS, *Standing cupid
with grapes*, detail of the
coopers' altar, now part of
the high altar, 1677-1678

PETER VERBRUGGHEN II,
The Birth of Mary, fragment of
the predella of the hosiers'
altar, 17th century

Verbrugghen I made a new altar for the guild of Our Lady of Praise in 1678. It was restored to the old design after the French Revolution, using mainly the original parts. About two years later Lodewijk Willemsens made a wooden communion rail for this altar. It is now to be found in St. Anthony's chapel.

The most impressive seventeenth-century piece of carved work in the cathedral is the organ cabinet above the west door. It belonged to one of the four baroque organs that the church had the good fortune to own and its original position was above the south entrance to the choir aisle. The cabinet and carvings were designed by Erasmus Quellin II, the cabinet was made by Michiel Bourgeois and the carvings were made by Peter Verbrugghen I in 1657. The organist at that time was Hendrik Liberti, who had succeeded the famous organist John Bull.

WILLEM KERRICX, *The raising up of the bronze serpent*, predella of the high altar, detail, 1734

ARTUS QUELLIN THE ELDER, *The Visit of Mary to her niece Elisabeth*, fragment of the altar of Our Lady of Praise, 1678

Photo right:
The baroque Schijven organ, cabinet and carving designed by ERASMUS QUELLIN II, paintings by PETER VERBRUGGHEN I, 1667

WILLEM KERRICX, *The raising up of the bronze serpent*, predella of the high altar, detail, 1734

Hendrik Liberti was also well-known and had been offered the post of court organist in 1635, but he had decided to remain in Antwerp (with a rise in salary). One of the main duties of organists had always been to accompany the choristers during the many services held in the church. Liberti had himself been a chorister before taking over from John Bull as organist of the Church of Our Lady. Choristers were singers who sang in the ordinary choir in return for board, lodging and schooling. A choirmaster was responsible for them and lived with them in the choir house that had been bought and established in 1421. Sometimes they were recruited from the boys in the city boys orphanage. The choir already had a long history in Liberti's day. There are references to choristers in the cathedral going back as far as 1362. In 1410 there had been eight choristers, supplemented when funds permitted by twelve professional singers so that the choir could sing the new polyphonic music. The most well-known name on the list of singers is undoubtedly that of Jan Ockegem, who was a member of the choir in 1443-1444. Ockegem gained fame above all as a composer of many masses, motets and songs. He was later employed by the king of France as a singer and director of music. The most famous choirmaster was probably Jacob Obrecht who composed 23 masses as well as a number of motets and songs. He worked in Antwerp from 1492. The religious disputes which were to lead in the following century to the destruction of the images and Calvinist control of the city were certainly not favourable conditions for nourishing the cathedral's rich musical tradition. Andries Pevernage was able to set matters to rights. He was choirmaster from 1585 until his death in 1591. He was a highly prolific composer and influenced figures such as Willem de Fesch and Joseph-Hector Fiocco.

Artus Quellin the Elder and Lodewijk Willemsens, *The mystical wine press*, detail of the coopers' altar, now part of the high altar, 1677-1678

In the eighteenth century there was a marked loss of interest in building and rebuild-ing altars, altar enclosures and epitaphs in the church. There were many reasons for this development, not least the intense activity of the previous centuries. The fervour of the Counter-Reformation had diminished as well, as Roman Catholicism won back its position. But it still had to be defended against beliefs such as Jansenism, named after Cornelius Janse-nius, a bishop and theologian from Ypres. Jansenius hoped that his study of the writings of Saint Augustine, a Father of the Church, would contribute to the restoration of Catholicism after the Council of Trent. When the Roman Curia condemned a number of his opinions, Jan-senius and the Jansenists turned out to be opponents of Rome's policy of centralization and

UNKNOWN ARTIST, *Jacobus Thomas Josephus Wellens, seventeenth bishop of Antwerp*

73

gave unambiguous support to tenets such as freedom of conscience in preference to obedience
to the rule of the Church. There was also another more insidious danger which threatened to
undermine the power and authority of the Church. If the strongest trend in the spiritual development of the sixteenth century had been the rise of humanism, and in the seventeenth century the Counter-Reformation, then the eighteenth century was the era of rationalism which
pronounced a new religion with the infallibility of the human mind as its central dogma and
taught unswerving faith in an ideal society which would be achieved with the help of science
and technology. The rise of secularism had begun. Church and State were divided. The
Enlightenment argued for an independent morality, not bound to religion. The Church in
contrast continued to see life on earth as a preparation for eternal life, but was swimming

against the tide. The universal church had to give ground and become a church for its believers in a secular society in which there was less social pressure to live a godly life. Obligatory and universal Christianity broke down and the state took over some of the areas in which the Church had been active: education, care of the poor... In the Treaty of Rastatt the Spanish Low Countries were given to Austria and our country was governed by Karl VI (1713-1740), Maria-Theresa (1740-1780) and Jozef II (1780-1790). Under these emperors and their governors the Enlightenment spread to the Austrian Low Countries and its effects were felt throughout society and in religious life. The authorities became increasingly involved in the affairs of the bishops of Antwerp, but for the time being their appointments were not affected.

Bishop Wellens had gained a reputation as a fervent defendant of the Roman faith even before his appointment to the see of Antwerp. As a native citizen of Antwerp he knew very well that Diderot, Voltaire and Rousseau were avidly read here. He owned a copy of Diderot's 'Encyclopédie' and the sciences were well represented in his library. The bishop was certainly not an opponent of science; he in fact had a keen interest in it, but was convinced that religion had a social dimension and defended broad pastoral concerns. When he took up his office it was clear that the citizens of Antwerp were not simply pleased that one of their own was to be their bishop; one of the street posters adorning the city was a chronogram:

Men DIscoUreert oVeraL Van WeLLens.
DIen WeLLens Is WaerlYk De geLeerthYd zelF
WeLLens zaL Die VoLtaIrIstJens botMUYLen.

which can be translated as:

Wellens is famous everywhere
Wellens is a very learned man
Wellens will shut the Voltairists up.

In contrast to Wellens, his successor Nelis was suspected (at least) of being too favourably inclined towards the French and English thinkers; it was also clear that he enjoyed the confidence and support of the Austrian authorities. Clerical circles in Antwerp were much less enthusiastic at his appointment than they had been about Bishop Wellens. It was thought that he was a pawn of Emperor-Verger Jozef II and of his plans for a State Church. However, while he was in office he was a resolute opponent of state interference in religious affairs. In 1785 the government decided that local seminaries would close and all priests would in future be trained in Leuven (Louvain). Nelis put up strong resistance to the implementation of this decision and to the closure of the Antwerp seminary which had been founded by his predecessor, Bishop Wellens. The authorities were forced to call in the troops to carry out the decision and the bishop was held under arrest in his episcopal palace for a few days. There was an unsuccessful attempt to take him prisoner in Brussels, where he had been summoned by the government, and he then went into voluntary exile for a few months. He did not return to Antwerp until 1790.

The belief of the Enlightenment that progress would come about through 'modern' science and industrial rationalism was not limited to calls for reform in the political arena and religious domain; the arts were also affected. In the early days Antwerp could still rely on its

G. VANDERHECHT,
*View of the nave with the triptych
by Peter Paul Rubens, Descent
from the Cross*, coloured
lithography

old baroque glories, but the focus of developments in the arts soon shifted to France. Flanders, which had been at the centre of things, decayed into a provincial backwater. Very few new and important works of art were created here. It was a very thin time for art in the cathedral.

The opposite pole to rationalism in philosophical terms was romanticism. This was a new movement with a strong interest in history, and therefore in Antwerp cathedral. In 1755 G. Berbie published his 'Description of the most important Paintings, Sculptures and other rarities from the hands of Famous Old Masters. Which are to be found in the Churches and Monasteries in the City of Antwerp... Published for the benefit of Travellers'. This book was a great success and was reprinted several times. In 1763 G.P. Mensaert wrote 'An enthusiastic and inquiring painter, or General description of the Paintings by the greatest Masters, which adorn the Churches, Monasteries, Abbies, Priories and Private apartments in the whole of the Austrian Low Countries'. Others were to follow, celebrating the rich artistic heritage to be found in Antwerp cathedral.

V isitors to the church today would not now find the guidebooks mentioned in the
previous chapter very useful. During the course of this book we have often said
that important works of art made for a particular altar are no longer in the church. The main
cause of their disappearance were the tumultuous events that shook the whole of Europe at the
end of the eighteenth century and the beginning of the nineteenth century. When the French
entered Antwerp for the first time in 1792 they were hailed by many as liberators who would
free them from the Austrians. There was nevertheless some fear of disorder, although the
French had promised to respect our constitution. Churchwarden Peter Jan Van Dyck noted in
his journal: "By half past eight in the evening all the emperor's coats of arms were removed
from the choir and the arms above the pew were painted over. On the following day, the 21st
of November 1792, the coat of arms above Saint Ursula was painted over, and the same was
done to all the coats of arms in blazons, altars, memorials and standing windows in the church
by order of the city and the chapter, so as to prevent any disturbance in the church since some
soldiers had been there a few days before, threatening with their swords and making signs that
these things should be taken out of the church."

The witch hunt was not directed just at coats of arms and blazons that were symbols of
the nobility and its power under the old regime. Attacks were also made on religion. Colonel
de Verrières tried to force bishop Nelis, a skilled diplomat, to commit himself. He invited him
to make an announcement in church, calling the people to a gathering that would create a
'société des droits de l'homme' [a society founded on human rights]. The priest tried to use
the convenient argument that the French had recently forbidden the clergy to dabble in poli-
tics and refused to cooperate. Shortly afterwards the occupying forces had an inventory of the
church's property made with a view to possible confiscation, but for the time being nothing
was taken. The Austrian regime was returned to power for a short time in April 1793. One
year later the French were once again at the gates of the city. On the 21st of July 1794 the
bishop left his residence and was never to return. A few days later French troops entered Ant-

Interior view, looking west

werp for the second time. The occupying forces exacted a levy on the city under threat of pillage and fire raising. The first 'contribution' was for one million, of which the chapter provided 7,115 guilders, but this was small beer in comparison to the demand for 10 million that was to follow. The churchwardens, the chapter, the chapels and the canons made personal contributions amounting to more than 330,000 pounds. To start with the contributions were paid in cash as far as possible, then with coupons and IOUs, but in the end the church had to give up some of its silver and gold works of art. Chalices, ciboria and altar plates disappeared into the revolutionary melting pot.

At around this time Lieutenant J.L. Barbier of the 5th Regiment of the French Hussars, himself a portrait painter, presented himself to seize the best works of art in Antwerp in the name of Peoples' Representative Richard. It had been his task before the capture of the city to look for art treasures in the conquered regions. Valuable paintings, and especially the works of Peter Paul Rubens, were to be removed from the churches and taken to Paris. Accompanied by French soldiers for protection, Barbier went to the cathedral, which had been closed for a few days for practical reasons, and had the *Descent from the Cross* with its side panels, the epitaphs to the Moretus, Goubau and Michielsen families taken down and prepared for the journey. As well as these paintings by Rubens, the French forces also took works by Rubens' master Otto van Veen, Wenzel Coeberger and Simon de Vos. On his arrival in Paris the abductor received a hero's welcome and made a remarkable speech. He said: 'Les ouvrages immortels que nous ont laissés les pinceaux de Rubens, de Van Dyck et les autres fondateurs de l'école flamande ne sont plus dans une terre étrangère. Réunis avec soin par les représantants du peuple, ils sont aujourd'hui déposés dans la patrie des arts et du génie, dans la patrie de la liberté et de l'égalité sainte, dans la République française'. [The immortal works left to us by the brush of Rubens, of Van Dyck and the other founders of the Flemish school are no longer on foreign soil. Gathered with care by the representatives of the people, they are today in the land of arts and of genius, in the land of liberty and holy equality, in the French Republic]. The notary P. De Decker had already heard similar comments on the lips of French soldiers in Antwerp, although they put it rather less pompously: 'les saints des églises belges n'avaient pas plutôt recouvré la liberté qu'ils ont voulu aller voir la Convention nationale'. [As soon as the saints of the Belgian churches got their freedom they wanted to go and see the National Convention]. After his triumphant return to Paris Barbier had got the taste and one month later he was back in Antwerp to take more works of art from the churches. The cathedral lost the *Assumption of the Virgin Mary* by Rubens, the *Fall of the rebellious angels* by Frans Floris, the *Last Judgement* by Jacob de Backer and the painting with the *Men of Emmaus* by Antonio Garibaldi. Later on the coat of arms of the Knights of the Golden Fleece, which had adorned the choir of the church for three hundred years, were removed to be burnt on a scaffold in public as a symbol of the old order.

It was not just works of art that were under threat; the clergy themselves were in danger. At the end of September 1795 they were forced to swear the Republican oath if they wished to continue in office. Churches with priests that had not sworn the oath but continued to hold services had to close. A few days later our provinces became part of the French Republic. French laws took effect here and contained provisions for the abolition of monasteries, guilds and corporations. Their possessions were seized. At the end of 1797 the laws were made more severe: all 'outward signs' of religion had to be removed from churches, streets and squares. The clergy had to swear opposition to the monarchy. If they did not do so their churches would be closed. As nobody took the oath, services were suspended and the churches were

JAN BLOM, *Cross-section of the transept and crossing,* drawing, Butchers' Guild Hall

closed. Property that had not yet been stolen was to be sold to the highest bidder at public auction. The chapter's fifty-eight houses and the church's one hundred and thirty-six houses, the farmland, gardens and meadows owned by the prebendary, the chaplains and the choristers and the works of art still in the church were to be sold. Citizens occupied the cathedral and started to clear it out. Some of them may have acted in this way in the hope of saving some of the treasures that had been placed in the church at great cost to honour God and adorn His house. Citoyen Roché tried to stop them but was attacked in the cathedral and died of his wounds three days later.

At the end of January 1798 two cathedral chaplains took the oath, hoping that they would then be allowed to open the church again. One of them collapsed on taking the oath, as if struck by the hand of God, and died on the spot. In the following month plans were made to capture the priests who had not sworn the oath and take them away. The priests who had taken the oath were still trying to have the churches opened. A former chaplain of the cathedral, J.A. Mortelmans, received permission to open St. James' church and hold services there. Jan Mertens, formerly pastor of Hoboken, had taken the oath and asked for the Church of Our Lady to be re-opened. The Commissioner of the Antwerp Executive Directoire, M. Dargonne, thought that there was no justification for opening the cathedral since attendance at services in the churches that were open was very low. He considered that the only reason for the request was that the population feared that the churches, 'ces monuments de la dévotion de leurs pères' [these monuments to the devotion of their fathers] would be destroyed. For these reasons he refused to re-open the cathedral. Dargonne, himself a landscape painter, was however in favour of the church and its art treasures being preserved as a monument. He suggested turning the former cathedral into a local museum. A commission had already been established to select works of art and science from churches, monasteries and other bodies which were to be preserved, i.e. not to be sold as property of the State but kept for the Ecole Centrale du Département des Deux-Nèthes, the school which replaced the Academie. 'Sale days' were held in the cathedral on the 15th of November 1798 and the following days. The items reserved by the commission were stored in a temporary museum, and most of the remainder were sold at ridiculously low prices. Many citizens did not dare to make a bid or did not want to bid. Many items were bought by foreigners, for example J.B. Adnet from Brussels who paid just three hundred guilders for the high altar and the tombs of the bishops (except for the tomb of Ambrosius Capello that had been chosen for the museum). When he tried to have his purchase loaded, the crane operators went on strike and had to be forced to move the pieces.

The church itself was in just as much danger as its furnishings. 'Ce temple est immense et ne peut être considéré comme un monument précieux qu'à cause des matériaux qui le composent' [This church is vast and can be considered a precious monument only because of the materials used in its construction]. It would be better to demolish the church to make room for enlargement of the 'place de l'égalité' [Liberty Square], the old churchyard. In the middle of this square a monument to the late Citoyen Roché could be erected. City architect Jan Blom was commissioned to survey the church. He started the work but did not make rapid progress. Either he had injured his thumb and was unable to draw, or the damp air of the church was bad for his frail health. Blom was still working on the plans when Napoleon's coup d'état replaced the Directoire with a Consulate that had a more tolerant attitude towards religion. A decree was issued to the effect that church buildings which had not been sold should be re-opened. However, the central administration feared that the people would riot when they saw

the damage that had been done to the interior of the cathedral in the meantime and claimed that the building was unsafe and could not be opened for that reason. The situation was only resolved by the appointment of Prefect d'Herbouville. He confirmed that the church would open again on his own authority and on condition that the building was first restored to a fit state at the churchwardens' expense. The commission to carry out the necessary work was given to none other than Jan Blom. After the rubble had been cleared away, thoughts turned to restoration in April 1800. The only items that had not been removed were the great organ above the choir aisle and the altar of the Young Archers' Guild, along with thirteen large and four small marble columns, a group of figures from the Chapel of Our Lady, some black marble steps, the door to the great sacristy, two altar tombs, two half-pillars and eight whole pillars of the choir rood loft, four white marble columns and some large blocks of black marble from the Venerable chapel, together with some small pillars and the marble enclosed porch in the south transept arm. These had been sold but the purchasers had never collected them. They were bought back, as were a number of other articles that had been removed from the church, and used in the restoration. Some other pieces were sold. A number of purchasers gave their acquisitions back to the church. Some works of art from other churches also found their way to the cathedral. The lands of the ancient Abbey of Saint Michael were turned into ship-

ARTUS QUELLIN THE ELDER, *Saint Anthony of Padua*, ca. 1675

yards as part of Napoleon's plan to make Antwerp into a 'pistol aimed at the heart of England'. Some of the abbey buildings were demolished and others were put to a different use. The famous abbey church became a warehouse. The floor stones were used to raise and restore the floor of the cathedral. The images of Saint Peter and Saint Paul from the choir rood loft in St. Michael's church were also sent to the cathedral. The Venerable altar was bought back and is still in use today in the Chapel of Saint Anthony, although the sculpture of St. Anthony in the altar came from the former minor friars' cloister which became an academy. The wonderful pulpit made in 1713 by Michiel Van der Voorts was bought from St. Bernard's Abbey in Hemiksem along with six confessionals and a communion rail. The Church of the Carmelites returned the oak communion rail that had originally been in the Chapel of Our Lady in the cathedral. A magnificent bronze crucifix from the Meir was donated to the cathedral. Fourteen of the works of art that had been reserved for the Ecole Centrale were returned, including the marble memorial to Bishop Capello and Frans Francken's altarpiece of *Jesus at the age of twelve among the scribes*. However, seventeen altarpieces that had been removed from the cathedral never returned. They had originally been taken to the Exchange where they were used as examples and educational material for future artists studying at the academy. In 1810 they were moved to the former minor friars' cloister where, together with many other works of art, they were to form the nucleus of the present-day Royal Museum of Fine Art. The guilds which had been the original owners were still dissolved and did not restore their altars.

Photo left:
Michiel van der Voort,
Pulpit, 1713

Figure of Christ in bronze
from the Meir, 1635

The great Rubens paintings that were the glory of Antwerp were still in Paris at this time, despite attempts to have them returned. Even a Frenchman on a visit to the city, A. Camus, regretted their absence: 'Il y a dix ans, j'ai vu la cathédrale d'Anvers; j'y avais admiré les chefs-d'œuvres de Rubens... Cette église aujourd'hui est entièrement nue... En considérant la place où j'avais longtemps fixé les yeux sur la belle Descente de croix de Rubens, je n'ai pu m'empêcher de dire: Puisqu'on ne pouvait transporter avec le tableau ni ce mur élevé sur lequel il se développait à l'aise avec ses volets, ni cette grande croisée, qui lui donnait le jour sous lequel il avait été dessiné, ni ce silence majestueux d'une vaste église qui préparait à l'étonnement et à l'admiration; que ne laissait-on entier à Anvers le chef-d'œuvre de Rubens que d'en transporter à Paris la moitié seulement?' [Ten years ago I saw Antwerp cathedral and admired the masterpieces by Rubens... This church is now entirely bare... When I look at the spot where I had spent so long in contemplation of Rubens' beautiful Descent from the Cross, I cannot help saying: Since it was not possible to take with the painting either the high wall on which it could spread at ease with its panels, or the great crossing which gave it the light in which it was painted, or the majestic silence of a vast church preparing the visitor for astonishment and admiration; would it not have been better to leave Rubens' masterpiece whole in Antwerp instead of taking only half of it to Paris?]. Walter Scott thought that the citizens of Antwerp had deliberately left empty and bare the place where the Descent from the Cross had previously hung so that they would not forget their great loss. But nothing could be further from the truth. They made every effort to recover what was theirs, exploiting every possible opportunity. Paris had received many more plundered works of art than could be accommodated in the Central Museum, but attempts to have works that were not intended for the museum returned to the Ecole Centrale in Antwerp were unsuccessful. When the departmental museums were created in 1802, Antwerp lost out once again. It is true that Napoleon donated 15,000 francs 'pour servir aux réparations de léglise d'Anvers' [to be used for repairs to Antwerp church] when he visited the city in 1803, but the paintings did not return.

Interior view from the Venerable chapel

The return of the stolen paintings and the restoration of the cathedral

After the battle of Waterloo the Belgian provinces were attached to the Kingdom of the Netherlands and came under the authority of Willem I, who had himself been very hard hit by the removal of works of art from the royal cabinet in The Hague. The members of the Antwerp Société Royale pour l'Encouragement des Beaux-Arts asked him to use his influence to have the lost works returned to Antwerp. England also saw the benefits of returning the paintings, though for other reasons. Lord Liverpool wrote to the English Consul in Paris that: 'Il est très désirable, au point de vue politique, de les faire sortir du territoire français; car tant qu'elles y resteront, elles ne peuvent manquer de faire vivre dans la nation française le souvenir de ses anciennes conquêtes et d'entretenir son esprit militaire et sa vanité' [It is highly desirable on political grounds to have them removed from French soil; since as long as they remain in France they will inevitably remind the French nation of its former conquests and nourish its military spirit and its vanity]. As the Antwerp city librarian Ger Schmook was later to comment, an artistic Waterloo had to be won at whatever cost. Soon afterwards a representative of the king and a commission of Antwerp citizens went to the French capital to locate the stolen works of art and bring them safely home. The mission was not without its difficulties, since as a member of the commission named Ommeganck wrote in a letter from Paris to his wife in Antwerp: 'You can imagine that the French are doing all they can to keep them... because if we start to take them back there will be such a void in the museum that uninformed visitors will think that the whole museum is being moved'. But the commission managed to take possession of most of the pieces and on 31 October a convoy bearing most of the works of art that had been stolen from Antwerp set off home. Some pieces were missing; these had already been sent from Paris to other museums in France where they remain to this day. The cathedral did not recover a painting of *Saint Sebastian* by Wenzel Coeberger painted for the altar of the Guild of Saint Sebastian which is now in Nancy museum; the *Epitaph of the Goubau family* by Rubens, now in Tours; a *Resurrection* by De Vos in Lille and a *Family Group* by the same artist which is now in Nantes.

The return to Antwerp of paintings taken to Paris during the French Revolution, 1816

Altar of Our Lady of Praise,
reconstructed after the
French Revolution with the
original pieces by ARTUS
QUELLIN THE ELDER and
PETER VERBRUGGHEN I,
1678 and 1825

WILLEM JACOB HERRYNS,
Christ and the Men of Emmaus,
1808

Antwerp knew that the long-awaited paintings were on their way back and planned a great celebration. The reception committee would have liked to see them brought back by boat on the river, with 'one particular painting taken out of its case and openly displayed in full sight of the people, if the weather permitted, and then put on a magnificent coach and brought into the city'. But reason prevailed over such enthusiasm and the masterpieces were brought in on a cart in closed boxes and taken to the minor friars' cloister for inspection. The Gazette van Braband reported: 'They are back. At about one o'clock on the fifth of December our long-awaited paintings arrived through the St. Joris Gate as the cannon fired and all the bells in the city rang out. They were received by the Mayor and his deputies, the City Council, the Board of the Academy and the Board of the Society for Promotion of the Arts, the students of the Academy, the churchwardens of churches that had claimed the paintings, the military authority and many troops and musicians; the paintings, loaded on four carts, travelled along the Gasthuisstraet, Huydevettersstraet, towards the Schoenmarkt, Oude Koordemerkt and stopped on the Groote Merkt in front of the Town Hall...' From there they were taken to the minor friars' cloister where they were hung by the 'unpacking committee' and then presented to the public for an admission charge of three francs. It seemed that the artistic Waterloo was won, and few people were disappointed that the planned procession was cancelled due to rainy weather. Jan Frans Willems wrote a poem on the subject of the paintings' return: 'Triumph! Antwerp! Rejoice!/ Your beautiful paintings/ Plundered by the French/ Torn from your Altars for twenty years/ have at last come home'.

P.P. Rubens,
Raising of the Cross, 1610

After restoration the *Descent from the Cross* and the *Assumption* were returned to the cathedral in 1816, along with the *Last Judgement* by Jacob de Backer. Rubens' *Resurrection of Christ* was returned to the Moretus family on the express condition that it would be displayed in the church. Frans Floris' *Fall of the rebellious angels* and Rubens' *Christ in the hay* were given to the museum in return for the glorious triptych of the *Raising of the Cross*. This painting had come from the high altar of St. Walburga's church but could not be sent back there as the church was now in ruins.

In this way the cathedral gradually regained some of its former splendour. The guild altars were not to be restored, but some of the old religious fraternities were resurrected and new ones were founded. The temporary altar that had been put up by the Guild of Our Lady of Praise for the re-opening of the church was replaced in 1825 by a marble altar of the same design as the old altar which had been lost during the revolution. Many of the original parts were used in its construction. Jacob Jan van der Neer had built a new neoclassical altar for the Venerable chapel two years earlier. The painting of *Christ and the men of Emmaus* that had been painted by Willem Jacob Herreyns in 1808 for the temporary altar in this chapel was kept for the new altar. Work was also being done on a new high altar. The churchwardens had bought

the old high altar of St. Walburga's church and parts of this altar together with columns from the former high altar of the abbey church in Tongerlo that had been bought in 1805 and parts of the old coopers' altar were used by Jan Blom to create a new high altar. The old organ from the transept was moved to a new west rood loft.

Following the old tradition, memorials once again started to appear in the church. Many of these were for members of the Moretus family. The memorials to the spouses Plantin-Rivière and Plantin-Moretus were put up again and a copy of Rubens' *Christ in the hay*, now in the museum, was painted for the De Pret-Moretus family. Louis Moretus commissioned a monumental crucifix from Jacob van der Neer, who also created a statue of *Saint Barbara* for the fraternity devoted to her. At around the same time a great silver-gilt solar monstrance by Jan-Baptist Verbeckt and a silver anointment lamp in Empire style were bought to replace the gold and silver articles that had been lost.

All these new works of art were made in the familiar late baroque and neoclassical style that had become popular towards the end of the eighteenth century, but in 1814 voices were raised in favour of producing neo-Gothic art for the cathedral. The principal champion of this view was the mayor of the city, Van Ertborn. He was a passionate enthusiast for Gothic art, and his collection included works by Jan van Eyck, Joos van Cleve, Ambrosius Benson, Dierick and Albrecht Bouts, Lucas Cranach, Gerard David, Jean Foucquet, Hans Memlinc, Quentin Metsys, Barend van Orley and Rogier van der Weyden. Van Ertborn's main argument in favour of neo-Gothic art was that there would then be a unity of style with the Gothic architecture of the building. In 1824, when the new high altar designed by Jan Blom was built, Van Ertborn's views were echoed by the lawyer and antiquarian Th. Van Lerius. But their arguments found little favour and the altar was made in the neoclassical style. The first neo-Gothic piece in the church were the new choir stalls designed by the architect Durlet in 1839. The design was the result of a competition in which the twenty-three year old Durlet took part along with older colleagues trained in the neoclassical style. Durlet was to play an important part in further work on the restoration of the cathedral. He was employed as the restoration architect from 1844 up until his death in 1867, and understandably turned to the new style as soon as he took up his post. As well as the concern to achieve unity of style, there was also the view that the Gothic was pre-eminently a religious style of art. It was thought that Gothic art dated from a time when religion still played a dominant part in society, and the neo-Gothic style was supported for this reason by the new Catholic revival and the growing number of influential Catholics. Work started on the new choir stalls in 1840 but had not yet been completed by the time of Durlet's death. The woodcarvers who had worked on them included Jozef Geefs, Karel Geerts, Jos Ducaju, Jean-Baptist de Cuyper, Jean-Baptist de Boeck and Jean-Baptist van Wint. They all enjoyed great renown from this and other commissions, including the new chapels surrounding the choir. Van Wint carved a monumental polychrome retable for Saint Joseph's chapel, inspired by the Late Gothic retables for which Antwerp had always been famous. He also made a similar carved retable with painted panels for the chapel of Saint Vincent a Paolo. He worked with De Boeck on a retable for the chapel of the Sacred Heart of Mary. Painted retables were made for the chapels of Saint Jan Berchmans, Saint Barbara and Saint Luke. These chapels were thoroughly renovated: repainted in neo-Gothic style and fitted with stained glass windows in a similar style. But the Gothic revival in the second half of the nineteenth century was not accepted by everyone: a number of classical designs were submitted to a competition held in 1854 for rood lofts in the transept, but a neo-Gothic design was se-

Photo right:
Woman in chains, detail of the choir stalls

The chapel of Saint Jan Berchmans with altar by J.F. DECKERS and altarpiece by P. VAN DER OUDERAA, 1889-1890

The chapel of Saint Barbara with altar by F. BAECKELMANS and altarpiece by J. ANTHONY, 1891

Photo right:
JEAN-BAPTIST DE BOECK
and JEAN-BAPTIST VAN
WINT, *Saint Joseph's retable*,
1871

lected. A few years later Durlet himself was commissioned to build a neo-Gothic altar to replace the high altar of 1824. This project was never brought to fruition. There was a considerable amount of opposition to the idea that the church should be repainted in bright colours. The old paintings from the fifteenth and sixteenth centuries had been painted over with whitewash in many parts of the church at the end of the sixteenth century, and the choir aisle and chapels surrounding the choir suffered the same fate, to loud protests, in 1695. The old paintings were rediscovered at the end of the eighteenth century when a fresh coat of whitewash was being applied, but no immediate action was taken. Around the middle of the nineteenth century work in the choir aisle revealed parts of the paintings once again. Argument raged back and forth as to whether the interior of the church should be again decorated with coloured paint. The supporters of this view pointed to examples of churches in Lier, Herentals, Brussels and Bruges. Finally a compromise was agreed: the chapels surrounding the choir would be painted in this way and the rest of the church would be left whitewashed. The chapel of God's Distress (1866-1867) and St. Joseph's chapel (1871-1872) had already been decorated in the neo-Gothic style. The chapel of Saint Luke and the chapel of Saint Vincent a Paolo followed in 1894 and 1897-98 respectively.

Work started on an important series of neo-Gothic stained glass windows in 1856 when the Royal Society for Encouragement of the Arts commissioned Jean-Baptiste Bethune to make a window in commemoration of the four hundredth anniversary of the foundation of the Guild of Saint Luke, the artists' guild. The window was to be placed above the south door and represent *God glorified by the arts, guilds and sciences.* Before this window was ready, another new window was made by the glazier Capronnier (1867), depicting Saint Peter and Saint Paul.

E. DIDRON, Stained glass
window with *Saint Norbert
restoring the worship of the Holy
Sacrament in Antwerp*, 1872

E. Didron, Stained glass window with *Saint Amand preaching the Gospel in Antwerp*, 1872

STALINS and JANSSENS,
Stained glass window with
*Alexander Farnese handing the keys
to the city to Our Lady*, 1884

New windows for the south side aisle were ordered from the firm of Didron in Paris. In 1872 the firm produced a *Saint Norbert restoring the worship of the Holy Sacrament in Antwerp* and *Saint Amand preaching the Gospel in Antwerp*. The first of these windows came in for some particular criticism as it represented the saint who had been in Antwerp in 1124 standing in front of the west facade of the church, which was not built until the fifteenth century, beside the well, which had been placed there only recently but had originally stood on the main square. It was obvious that the French artist had taken great liberties with Antwerp's history. Stinging polemics appeared in the art journals of the day, and some satirical pamphlets were published. To avoid further dispute it was decided that the windows which were to be placed on the opposite side would be designed by Pieter van der Ouderaa. He was a member of the cathedral's Commission for Art and Archeology, which carried out historical research and advised the board of churchwardens accordingly before any work was done. They looked into subjects such as *The veneration of Our Lady of the Branch* and *Alexander Farnese handing the keys to the city to Our Lady in 1585*. Most of these windows were made by the Antwerp firm Stalins & Janssens, local people rather than foreigners. Neo-Gothic stained glass windows, most of them made by Bethune or Stalins & Janssens, were also put up in the chapels surrounding the choir.

Restoration of the building had now started after the most urgent repairs had been carried out. Work was done on the great tower between 1833 and 1865, moving on to the south tower, the west front, the transept, sections of the choir and the church doors from 1844 up till 1917. The view at the time was that the restorers were taking a very imaginative approach to their work and made the church look more 'Gothic' than it had been before. Gothic balus-

West door with statues of saints who have played a part in Antwerp's history, 1897-1903

Photo right:
Sanctuary vault

trades appeared on the roof for the first time and statues were placed in the outer porches as was the practice in French cathedrals. A selection of saints who had played a part in the history of the Antwerp region appeared in the west porch: Eligius, Fredegandus, Walburga, Boniface, Dymphna, Willibrord, Amand and Norbert. A *Last Judgement* was placed in the tympan and a standing figure of Our Lady next to the pier. The archivolts were peopled with angels, apostles, founders of religious orders and Fathers of the Church.

The Royal Commission for Monuments, which supervised the actual restoration work, did not only give its approval for all of these innovations. In 1856 it also insisted on demolishing a number of small houses that had for centuries stood against the west side of the tower. The commission thought that they spoiled the view of the west front. Later on there were calls for a thorough 'clear-out' of the church, including the choir. To start with only two of the little houses in the adjoining Blauwmoezelstraat and the ones built against the west front were torn down. Eight houses perished when a sacristy for the Chapel of Our Lady was built. A couple more were lost during the restoration of the north transept and at the beginning of the twentieth century the battle between the 'degagistes' and the 'antidegagistes', groups for and against creating a clear view of the cathedral, flared up again and led to the demolition of two little houses on the south side of the church. But there was never a complete dismantling.

The two world wars did not cause much damage to the church but did delay important restoration work, which did not start again until after the revival of the diocese of Antwerp in 1961. In 1965 the provincial government decided that the whole building with the exception of the great tower should be thoroughly cleaned and restored. Work on the tower had started in the nineteen-twenties under the supervision of the city council, and it was decided that the work should be continued on this basis. As a great deal of work was necessary, both for the exterior of the building that had been damaged by wind and weather and for the interior which was in a filthy state, the project was divided into separate stages. Work started, logically enough, on repairing the roof and implementing fire safety precautions (1969-1972). Damage to the slates, to centuries-old oak rafters and gutters allowed rainwater through into the body of the church and was also at some points a potential hazard to the stability of the building. Once these repairs had been done, attention turned to restoration of the nave (1973-1983). When the pillars in the nave had been cleaned it became apparent how much damage had been caused by the fire in 1533. The intense heat had caused large pieces of the stone cladding of the columns to break up. This damage had been simply plastered over after the fire, but now proper repairs were carried out. All the old and dirty coats of paint were stripped off the stone, and air conditioning, lighting and amplifiers were installed. The work was then suspended for a while to allow archeologists and art historians to complete a thorough preparatory investigation of the site before the work continued, so that the right choices would be made in the next stages of the work. Archive sources and archaeological finds in the foundations and walls gave a more complete picture of the history of the building and

View of the nave with the damage caused to the pillars during the 1533 fire

the phases of its construction. The investigation confirmed the suspicion that church interiors like those of the cathedral had originally been painted. The appearance of the newly restored nave was therefore anything but historically correct. Many stages of the decorative work also indicated that the interior was not simply whitewashed all over, but that coloured paint had been used in many parts and there were some wall paintings of artistic and historical interest. Restoration of these wall paintings would however breach the unity of the church interior and would be a too dramatic change in approach. For this reason it was decided, more or less as in the nineteenth century, to keep the whitewash coat in the transept and sanctuary and to restore the colourful paintings dating from the fifteenth to nineteenth centuries only in the chapels surrounding the choir, as this would have less impact on the overall appearance of the church interior. Work was done on the transept and sanctuary between 1990 and 1993, and the next complex task is the restoration of the choir aisle and the chapels surrounding the choir. This work will start in 1994.

Archaeological excavations
1972-1983

The re-opening of the
cathedral after restoration on
the 3rd of April 1993

Photos: H. Maertens, © Provinciebestuur Antwerpen
        (except pp. 2, 3, 28, 86, 104, 113)
Drawings: © Provinciebestuur Antwerpen
Layout: Annick Blommaert
Photogravure and printing: Snoeck-Ducaju & Zoon
Translation: Patricia Jenner for Linguist Associates International

D/1994/0012/14
ISBN 90-5349-116-3